Complete English as a Second Language for Cambridge Secondary 1

ASPIRE
SUCCEED
PROGRESS

7

Chris Akhurst, Lucy Bowley, Lynette Simonis

Series editor: Rachel Beveridge

Oxford excellence for Cambridge Secondary 1

OXFORD

OXFORD
UNIVERSITY PRESS

Great Clarendon Street, Oxford, OX2 6DP, United Kingdom

Oxford University Press is a department of the University of Oxford. It furthers the University's objective of excellence in research, scholarship, and education by publishing worldwide. Oxford is a registered trade mark of Oxford University Press in the UK and in certain other countries

First published in 2016

British Library Cataloguing in Publication Data
Data available

978-0-19-837812-9

9 10

Paper used in the production of this book is a natural, recyclable product made from wood grown in sustainable forests.
The manufacturing process conforms to the environmental regulations of the country of origin.

Printed in Great Britain by Bell and Bain Ltd, Glasgow

Acknowledgements
The publishers would like to thank the following for permissions to use their photographs:

Cover image: Jenny Wheatley/Bridgeman Images; p8: NASA Photo/Alamy Stock Photo; p8: Sim Kay Seng/123RF; p9: NASA; p9: Mike Flippo/Shutterstock; p9: Deddeda/Design Pics/Getty Images; p10: Vadim Sadovski/Shutterstock; p11: age fotostock/Alamy Images; p12: Michelangelus/Shutterstock; p13: Elena Milevska/Fotolia; p13: Dieter Willasch/NASA; p13: iurii/Shutterstock Images; p13: donfiore/Shutterstock Images; p14: Zoonar GmbH/Alamy; p14: Boule/Shutterstock; p15: Volodymyr Goinyk/Shutterstock; p16: Jenny Zhang/Shutterstock; p16: carl/Fotolia; p16: Chris Laurens/Alamy Images; p16: Lukas Wydrzynski/EyeEm/Getty Images; p17: jaroslava V/Shutterstock; p18: blackday/Fotolia; p18: Tatiana Popova/Shutterstock; p18: qvist/Shutterstock; p18: Evan Lorne/Shutterstock; p18: tan4ikk/Fotolia; p19: Ute Averkamp/Getty Images; p21: Brenda Carson/123RF; p24-39: Stefan Schurr/Shutterstock; p24: Oleg66/Gettyimages; p24: PAUL BUCK/EPA/Newscom; p25: Dionisvera/Shutterstock; p25: Dusan Kostic/Fotolia; p25: Rodimovpavel/Fotolia; p26: Sam Kang Li/ASSOCIATED PRESS; p27: Jim West/Alamy Stock Photo; p27: Henry Browne/ZUMAPRESS/Newscom; p27: Shingo Ito/AFLO SPORT/Newscom; p30: Akihiro Sugimoto/Gettyimages; p30: Alfonso de Tomas/Shutterstock; p31: Hugh Routledge/REX Shutterstock/Newscom; p32: Andersen Ross/DigitalVision/Getty Images; p32: Juanmonino/Vetta/Getty Images; p32: Robert Niedring/Corbis; p32: Michael DeYoung/Blend Images/Getty Images; p36: Get Out Alive with Bear Grylls - Season 1.; p40-55: Filipe Frazao/Shutterstock; p40: Settawat Udom/Shutterstock; p40: Ndoeljindoel/Shutterstock; p41: Santypan/Shutterstock; p41: Wavebreakmedia/Shutterstock; p41: Iakov Filimonov/Shutterstock; p42: Sorbis/Shutterstock; p43: Fedor Selivanov/Shutterstock; p46: Murgermari/Shutterstock; p47: Igor Plotnikov/Shutterstock; p50: Lamarinx/Shutterstock; p50: India Picture/Shutterstock; p50: Kzenon/Shutterstock; p50: Monkey Business Images/Shutterstock; p50: Simone van den Berg/Shutterstock; p56-71: Carolyn Jenkins/Alamy Stock Photo; p56: Hero Images/Getty Images; p56: Oliveromg/Shutterstock; p58: ZAK Hussein/SIPA/Newscom; p62: Sutton-Hibbert/REX/Newscom; p66: Wavebreakmedia/Shutterstock; p66: Jacek Chabraszewski/Shutterstock; p66: wavebreakmedia/Shutterstock; p66: Joe McBride/The Image Bank/Getty Images; p68: tristan tan/Shutterstock; p69: Iurii Augulis/Shutterstock; p72-87: Alvindom/Shutterstock; p72: Monkey Business Images/Shutterstock; p72: Image Source/Getty Images; p82: Hero Images/Getty Images; p82: Catalin Petolea/Shutterstock; p82: THOMAS SAMSON/AFP/Getty Images; p82: Universal Images Group/Getty Images; p89-103: Operation Shooting/Shutterstock; p88: Klaus Vedfelt/Taxi/Getty Images; p88: Ricky Paras/Moment/Getty Images; p89: Kali9/E+/Getty Images; p89: Purestock/Getty Images; p90: Bill Bachman/Alamy Stock Photo; p91: Nigel Dickinson/Alamy Stock Photo; p94: Kaori Ando/Image Source/Getty Images; p95: Ahturner/Shutterstock; p100: Ossile/Shutterstock; p101: Nattika/Shutterstock; p104-119: Africa Studio/Shutterstock; p104: Jeff Schultes/Shutterstock; p104: Nosonjai/Shutterstock; p105: McCarthy's PhotoWorks/Shutterstock; p105: Marchesini62/Shutterstock; p106: Neil Setchfield/Alamy Stock Photo; p106: Monkey Business Images/Shutterstock; p107: Andresr/Shutterstock; p110: Peter Dazeley/The Image Bank/Getty Images; p111: Samot/Shutterstock; p114: Epa european pressphoto agency b.v./Alamy Stock Photo; p114: Jon Binalay creations/Moment/Getty Images; p114: CLAIRE TAKACS/Alamy Stock Photo; p114: epa european pressphoto agency b.v./Alamy Stock Photo; p114: WovenSouls Cultural Images/Alamy Stock Photo; p114: Mikadun/Shutterstock; p116: Adwo/Alamy Stock Photo; p117: LaMiaFotografia/Shutterstock; p120-135: MaraZe/Shutterstock; p120: Henk Badenhorst/E+/Getty Images; p120: Adisa/Shutterstock; p121: Eastimages/Shutterstock; p121: Africa Studio/Shutterstock; p121: Stephen VanHorn/Shutterstock; p122: Brenda Carson/Shutterstock; p130: Shakim888/Shutterstock; p130: Margouillat photo/Shutterstock; p130: Sebastian Duda/Shutterstock; p130: Diogoppr/Shutterstock; p131: Piyato/Shutterstock; p132: Artwork © Quentin Blake. Used by arrangement with Random House Children's Publishers UK, a division of The Random House Group Limited; p133: Philip Sayer/Alamy Stock Photo; p136-151: Babich Alexander/Shutterstock; p136: KidStock/Blend Images/Getty Images; p136: FooTToo/Shutterstock; p137: Lane Oatey/Blue Jean Images/Getty Images; p137: Andrey Armyagov/Shutterstock; p137: Artbox/Shutterstock; p138: NYPL NYPL/Science Source/Getty Images; p139: Everett Historical/Shutterstock.

Artwork by Aptara Inc. and Erwin Haya.

We are grateful to the authors and publishers for use of extracts from their titles and in particular for the following:

Bear Grylls: Interview for The Scout Association reprinted by permission of Peters Fraser & Dunlop (www.petersfraserdunlop.com) on behalf of Bear Grylls.

C.S. Lewis: THE LION, THE WITCH AND THE WARDROBE copyright © C.S. Lewis Pte. Ltd. 1950. Extract reprinted by permission.

Gill Lewis: Extract from *Sky Hawk* (OUP, 2011), text copyright © Gill Lewis 2011, reproduced by permission of Oxford University Press.

Jacqueline Wilson: Interview from https://clubs-kids.scholastic.co.uk/clubs. Reproduced by permission of David Higham Associates.

Star Chat: Into the Woods http://www.ngkids.co.uk/entertainment/star-chat-for-into-the-woods. Reprinted with permission of National Geographic Kids magazine, www.ngkids.co.uk.

Ten facts about space! http://ngkids.co.uk/science-and-nature/ten-facts-about-space. Reprinted with permission of National Geographic Kids magazine, www.ngkids.co.uk.

Contents

Introduction

Welcome to ***Complete English as a Second Language for Cambridge Secondary 1***. This Student Book is the first in a series of three books (Stages 7–9) and is mapped to the *Cambridge Secondary 1* curriculum framework for English as a Second Language.

Who is the book for?

The book has been written for learners of English as a second language and covers all five key skills of the framework: reading, writing, speaking, listening, and use of English. It is designed to meet you where you are and help you improve, with activities that increase gradually in difficulty. It also aims to prepare you to take the Cambridge Secondary 1 Checkpoint test at the end of Stage 9, and then go on to Cambridge IGCSE®.

What is in the book?

The book is divided into nine units, which cover a broad range of fun and interesting topics to give you a wide vocabulary. Each unit includes each of the key skills from the curriculum framework, using the same structure throughout.

Theme opener

Each unit starts with a diagram like the one below, which will show what is covered in that unit.

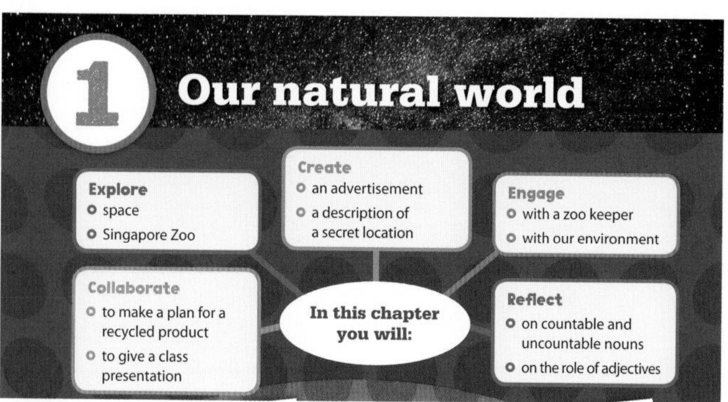

Photos and quotes help you to start thinking and talking about the topic, building some of the vocabulary that you will need throughout the unit.

Reading

You will find a broad range of writing styles and registers. Each text is followed by questions to make sure you have understood the text.

At the end of each unit, you will also find a 'Reading corner', which will introduce you to a slightly longer and more challenging text. This is designed to give you an appreciation of English in many different contexts and to help model good writing skills.

Use of English

You will find two sections on the use of English in each unit: these include short explanations on the grammar and punctuation rules that you will need to know, followed by activities to put into practice what you have learned.

Listening

Listening activities include different styles of talk and conversation, followed by questions, to help develop your understanding of spoken English. The audio recordings are on the CD in your book where you can also find transcripts (or the 'text' of what you hear) for extra help.

Speaking

You will have the chance to practise your speaking skills, both in groups and on your own. There will usually be a picture or photo, followed by discussion questions, to help get you started.

Writing

Short writing activities are scattered throughout the book and each unit includes one 'Writing workshop' in which you complete an extended piece of writing (100–120 words). This covers many different types of writing, such as stories, letters, reports and blogs.

Progress assessment

Each unit ends with a Progress check, a quick test to make sure that you have remembered what you learned in the unit. This is followed by a Progress assessment grid and an Action plan to help you decide where you need to improve.

Other features

World builder

Word builder: activities to help you understand and practise using difficult words.

Remember

Remember: short tips to remind you of things you have already learned, that will help you to complete the activities.

Challenge

Challenge: if you are feeling confident, the stretching Challenge activities provide extra practice.

Suggested reading

Suggested reading: if you like the extracts in the 'Reading corner', you will find suggestions for other texts that you might like.

Glossary

Glossary: really difficult words will have a definition (in English) to help you understand the text or listening task.

And finally...

We have included a very wide range of themes, texts and listening scenarios so we hope you will find this book interesting and engaging, as you grow into confident, responsible, reflective, innovative and engaged learners of English. Good luck!

Unit contents

Unit	Theme	Reading and comprehension	Listening and comprehension
1	Our natural world	Non-fiction: Ten facts about space! Fiction: adventure/description: *Sky Hawk*	Zoo keeper talks about her work at Singapore Zoo
2	Fit for life	Non-fiction: Report about The Youth Olympic Games Blog: Bear Grylls	Interview with a footballer
3	Work around the world	Informal letter: Letter to a friend about transport in Hong Kong Newspaper job advertisements	VSO volunteer describes his work in Nepal
4	Leisure	Interview: interview with a film actor (Star Chat: *Into the Woods*) Fiction: *The Lion, the Witch and the Wardrobe*	Interview with an author (Jacqueline Wilson)
5	Friends	Emails: emails between friends	Conversation between old friends
6	Where we learn	Non-fiction: The School of the Air Non-fiction: Online newspaper article	Radio broadcast: Learning new things every day
7	Culture and customs	Non-fiction: Birthday celebrations around the world Poetry: The Boab Festival	Mu Lan describes the preparations for Chinese New Year Interview: New Year celebrations
8	Cookbook	Recipe Review of a cookbook	Friends talk about different recipes
9	Communication	Non-fiction: The first telephone call	Four different kinds of signalling systems

Language, grammar, spelling, vocabulary	Writing	Speaking
Countable and uncountable nouns Determiners Quantifiers Compound adjectives Participle adjectives Comparative adjectives and comparative structures	Non-fiction: writing facts about space Non-fiction: writing an advertisement (persuasive language) Fiction: Descriptive writing	Expressing opinions Spoken presentation Speaking to persuade Expression of ideas Negotiating classroom tasks Using subject-specific vocabulary
Indefinite pronouns Quantitative pronouns Present perfect tense Proofreading and editing Language for discussions: asking and giving reasons and opinions	Non-fiction: writing a paragraph about sporting role model Writing a blog	Asking questions Expressing opinions Giving reasons for opinions Taking part in a role-play interview Class presentation
Active and passive present simple Causative forms (*have, get done*) Present continuous Past continuous	Letter: writing a formal letter Writing a persuasive paragraph Writing a letter to a friend Writing an advertisement for a school council position	Expressing opinions Organisation of ideas Role-playing a job interview Devising a spoken advertisement Class presentation
Comparative adverb structures Sentence adverbs (*too, either, also*) Pre-verbal, post-verbal and end position adverbs	Non-fiction: Writing a text message Non-fiction: Writing interview questions Playscript: writing a playscript	Expressing opinions Organisation of ideas Asking questions Using subject-specific vocabulary
Compound nouns Abstract nouns Gerunds as subjects and objects Noun phrases Determiners Proofreading and editing	Non-fiction: short paragraph about what makes a good friend Informal letter: writing an informal letter to a penfriend	Expressing opinions Using subject-specific vocabulary Negotiating classroom tasks Role-play an interview between old friends
Language for asking closed, open and rhetorical questions Modal verbs Conjunctions Informal and informal language	Non-fiction: Writing an online newspaper article	Expressing opinions Asking questions Using subject-specific vocabulary
Prepositions and prepositional phrases Conditional sentences, using 'If only' and 'wish'	Writing an invitation Writing an informal email Writing a description of a festival Writing a poem	Asking questions Role-play an interview Expressing opinions Using subject-specific vocabulary
Reported speech Determiners Present continuous Active and passive verbs	Writing a book review	Expressing opinions Asking questions Using subject-specific vocabulary
Verbs and adjectives, followed by infinitives *-ing* forms after verbs and prepositions Phrasal verbs Prepositional verbs	Writing a formal email (responding to an advertisement) Planning, writing, editing and proofreading	Class presentation Negotiating classroom tasks Expressing opinions Asking questions Using subject-specific vocabulary

1 Our natural world

Explore
- space
- Singapore Zoo

Create
- an advertisement
- a description of a secret location

Engage
- with a zoo keeper
- with our environment

Collaborate
- to make a plan for a recycled product
- to give a class presentation

In this chapter you will:

Reflect
- on countable and uncountable nouns
- on the role of adjectives

Time flies when flying at 28 800 km/h.
Tim Peake, astronaut

I like animals. I like natural history. The travel bit is not the important bit.
David Attenborough, naturalist and broadcaster

Look up at the stars and not down at your feet. Stephen Hawking, physicist

Thinking ahead

1. What can you see in the sky at night?
2. What is your favourite wild animal and why?
3. Why is it important to recycle things we no longer need?
4. Why do you think Stephen Hawking says you should look up at the stars rather than down at your feet?

Word builder

Use words from the word box to complete the sentences below.

environment	solar system	orbit
recycled	endangered	extinct

1. Earth is one of the planets that ______________ the sun.
2. The sun is a star at the centre of our ______________.
3. Some wild animals are in danger of becoming ______________.
4. Some zoos help to protect ______________ species.
5. Many waste products can be ______________.
6. Recycling helps to protect the ______________.

Speaking

Discuss the following questions with a partner. Remember to give reasons for your opinions.

1. Neil Armstrong was the first person to walk on the moon, in 1969. Would you like to be an astronaut and travel into space?
2. Some endangered wild animals, such as orangutans, are kept in zoos. What can zoos do to help them?
3. How does recycling waste products help to protect the environment?

Ten facts about space!

Read the following facts about space and then answer the questions.

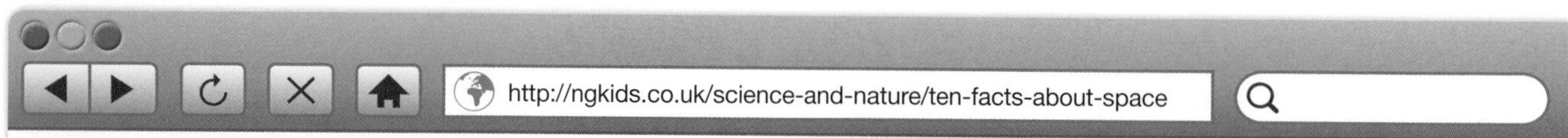

1. One million Earths could fit inside the sun – and the sun is considered an average-size star.
2. For years it was believed that Earth was the only planet in our solar system with liquid water. More recently, NASA revealed its strongest **evidence** yet that there is ... running water on Mars, too!
3. Comets are leftovers from the creation of our solar system about 4.5 billion years ago – they consist of sand, ice and carbon dioxide.
4. You **wouldn't be able to** walk on Jupiter, Saturn, Uranus or Neptune because they have no solid surface!
5. If you could fly a plane to Pluto, the trip would take more than 800 years!
6. Space junk is any human-made object orbiting Earth that no longer serves a useful purpose. Scientists estimate there are about 500,000 pieces of space junk today, including fragments from rockets and satellites, and everyday items like **spanners** dropped during construction of the International Space Station!

7. An **asteroid** about the size of a car enters Earth's **atmosphere** roughly once a year – but it burns up before it reaches us. Phew!
8. The highest mountain known to man is on an asteroid called Vesta. Measuring a **whopping** 22km in height, it is three times as tall as Mount Everest!
9. There are more stars in the universe than grains of sand on all the beaches on Earth. That's at least a billion trillion!
10. The sunset on Mars appears blue.

Understanding

A Answer the following questions.

1. What three things are comets made of?
2. How long would it take to travel to Pluto by plane?
3. How many pieces of space junk are orbiting Earth?
4. On Mars, what colour is the sunset?

Glossary

asteroid a rocky object that orbits the sun

atmosphere the gases surrounding a planet

evidence information that shows something is true

spanners tools used to make something tighter or looser

whopping huge

wouldn't be able to can't

B **Choose the correct answer to the following questions.**

1. What do the 'Ten facts about space' on page 10 provide for the reader?
   - **a** information about when the International Space Station was built
   - **b** factual information about the planets and other objects in our solar system
   - **c** an explanation of what an asteroid is
2. How are Jupiter, Saturn, Uranus or Neptune different from Earth?
   - **a** they have no liquid water
   - **b** they are outside the solar system
   - **c** they have a solid surface

C **Choose the correct answer to the following questions.**

1. Which one of the following statements is true?
   - **a** Our solar system contains millions of stars.
   - **b** Space junk has existed in our solar system for billions of years.
   - **c** Comets come from the time when the solar system was formed.
2. Which of these definitions is closest in meaning to the word 'fragments' in fact 6?
   - **a** leftovers from rockets and satellites
   - **b** small pieces or parts that have broken off something
   - **c** spanners and other human-made objects

Remember

Factual information often includes technical words. If you come across a word you do not understand, you may be able to guess its meaning from clues in the text or from the words that come before and after it.

Writing

Use the Internet and/or books in your library to find out more information about one of the planets in our solar system. Make some notes about what you find. Now, using the text on page 10 as a model, write five interesting facts about the planet you have chosen. When you have finished, compare your facts with those of a partner.

Speaking

Using the information and words you learned in the writing activity above, give a two-minute presentation to your classmates about the planet you found out about.

Countable and uncountable nouns

There are two types of noun: countable nouns and uncountable nouns.

Countable nouns name things we can count, such as 'fact', 'planet' and 'car'. To describe how many there are, we can use numbers.

Example: I have read **ten facts** about space.

Uncountable nouns name things we cannot count, such as 'information' and 'sand'. We cannot use numbers with uncountable nouns (we cannot say 'two sands').

Example: Comets contain **sand**.

We do not always use numbers with countable nouns. When there is just one, we can use the words 'a' or 'an'. When there is more than one, we can use the word 'some'.

Examples: The sun is **a star**.
Vesta is **an asteroid**.
I can see **some stars**.

With uncountable nouns, we cannot use the words 'a' or 'an' (we cannot say 'an information') but we can use the word 'some'.

Example: I have read **some information** about the planets.

Using countable and uncountable nouns 1

A Answer the following questions.

1. Which two of the following nouns are countable?

a comet

b scientist

c air

2. Which two of the following nouns are uncountable?

a water

b beach

c ice

B Complete the following sentences with the words 'a', 'an' or 'some'.

1. The sun is __________ star at the centre of our solar system.

2. There is __________ water in the glass.

3. __________ planets in our solar system are made of gas.

4. Vesta is __________ object that is orbiting the sun.

5. There is __________ sand in my shoe.

How many and how much?

With **countable nouns**, we can use numbers to say exactly how many there are of something. We can also use words such as 'both (of)', 'all (of)' and 'half (of)'. When we are being less exact, we can use the words 'many', 'few' and 'several' and phrases such as 'a small number of'.

Examples:

many years	**several** planets	**both** the scientists
a few mountains	**a small number of** comets	**half of** the water

With **uncountable nouns**, we can use 'a little', 'a lot' and 'much' to describe how much there is of something. We can also use phrases such as 'a large amount of' and 'plenty of' or 'a bottle of'.

Examples: **a little** information
a lot of sand
a large amount of money
plenty of air
a bottle of water

Using countable and uncountable nouns 2

A **Rewrite the following sentences, filling the gaps with the correct word or phrase from the box below.**

a large amount of   a few   many   plenty of

1. There are ______________ stars in the universe.
2. There is ______________ space junk orbiting the sun.
3. Only ______________ people have walked on the moon.
4. I have ______________ time to read about the planets.

B **Use a word or phrase from the box on the left and a word from the box on the right to describe each picture A, B, and C.**

a glass of		astronaut
a lot of	+	water
one		stars

C **Write four sentences of your own about the solar system using countable and uncountable nouns.**

Track 1.1: Singapore Zoo

Some animals live in the wild, some live in our homes and some live in zoos. In the recording, you will hear a zoo keeper describing her work at Singapore Zoo. Listen carefully and then answer the questions.

Understanding

A Read the following paragraph and fill each gap with the correct word from the four options in the list below.

I started working at Singapore Zoo **(1)** ______ years ago and they have been the best years of my life. It was a job I always wanted to have and I am so **(2)** ______ here. My favourite animals are the **(3)** _________, as they really seem to understand us humans. Visitors can come and start their day by having **(4)** __________ with the animals. It is a lot of **(5)** ________ but also reminds visitors to think about the animals for the rest of the day. At the moment, I am planning a new **(6)** ________ area for the monkeys, which will be really good and exciting for them. I am planning to add lots of **(7)** _________, which will make them **(8)** _______ as well as play, so it will be stimulating for them as well as enjoyable. They will **(9)** __________ it when it is finally finished. The thing I like the most about my job is being able to go home knowing endangered animals are being protected for the **(10)** _________.

1.	60	6	16	66
2.	sad	unhappy	happy	glad
3.	monkeys	orangutans	koalas	elephants
4.	breakfast	lunch	tea	dinner
5.	work	noise	fun	problems
6.	food	work	play	music
7.	pieces	sections	straw	food
8.	see	touch	look	think
9.	love	break	damage	touch
10.	zoo	visitors	plane	future

B For each question, choose the correct answer.

1. Why is the zoo keeper planning a new area for the monkeys?
   - **a** She wants the zoo to have more monkeys.
   - **b** She wants to give the monkeys more space to play and more to think about.
   - **c** She wants visitors to be able to see the monkeys more easily.
2. What does the zoo keeper like most about her job?
   - **a** spending time with the orangutans
   - **b** meeting the visitors
   - **c** helping to protect endangered animals

C Write a sentence to explain what the zoo keeper means when she says the following phrases.

1. it will be stimulating for them as well as enjoyable
2. endangered animals are being protected for the future

Writing

Singapore Zoo is a popular place to visit but needs to attract even more visitors. The zoo has asked you to produce an advertisement.

1. Decide on the format of your advertisement. For example, it could be an email that will be sent to animal lovers, a poster or a radio advertisement.
2. Note down a few reasons why people should go to Singapore Zoo.
3. Think of words and phrases to describe the zoo in a positive way. What words can you use to persuade people to visit?
4. Now write your advertisement.
5. Show the advertisement to your classmates. Can they suggest improvements?

Challenge

You have been given the power to save for all time one of the endangered species at Singapore Zoo. Decide which one you are going to save and why.

1. Choose an endangered animal that you know is kept at the zoo (check the website if you are not sure).
2. Research the animal to find out:
   - where it lives naturally
   - how many are still living in the wild
   - why it has become endangered
   - what is being done to protect it.
3. Give a two-minute presentation to your classmates, using words and phrases that will persuade them that the animal you have chosen should be saved.

Adjectives

Adjectives are used to describe or give more information about nouns. We use them to add detail and interest to what we are writing or talking about.

Example: Singapore has a **famous** zoo.

Some adjectives are made from more than one word. We call these **compound adjectives**. When a compound adjective comes before the noun, we usually use a hyphen (-) between the words.

Example: Singapore has a **world-famous** zoo.

Many adjectives end in –ed or –ing. We often use adjectives that end in –ed to describe feelings.

Example: We were **excited**.

We often use adjectives ending in –ing to describe things that cause the feelings.

Example: We had an **exciting** day.

Many compound adjectives include words ending in –ing or –ed.

Example: The **well-behaved** monkeys were waiting to be fed.

Using adjectives

A Using one word from each column in the box below, make four compound adjectives.

multi	speed
snow	coloured
sweet	covered
high	smelling

B Choose the correct adjectives to complete these sentences.

1. The zoo keeper has an ______________ job. (interested/ interesting)
2. I was ______________ to see so many giraffes. (surprising/ surprised)
3. I saw some ______________ white tigers. (endangering/ endangered)
4. The monkeys had an ______________ area to play in. (amazed/amazing)

C Use the compound adjectives you made in A to write a sentence describing each of the pictures A, B, C and D.

Comparative adjectives

To compare one person, animal or object with another, we use **comparative adjectives**. When we are comparing two things in a sentence, we often use the word 'than'.

Example: A giraffe is **taller than** a llama.

When an adjective has one syllable, we usually make a comparative by adding –er. When an adjective has two syllables or more, we usually use 'more'. When a two-syllable adjective ends in 'y', change the 'y' to 'i' and then add '–er'.

Examples: old ⟶ older   interesting ⟶ more interesting   happy ⟶ happier

To add more detail to what we say and write, we can also use phrases such as 'not as … as' and 'much … than'.

Examples: The llama is **not as tall as** the giraffe.   The giraffe is **much taller than** the llama.

Using comparatives

A Make comparative adjectives from the words below and then use them in the following sentences.

dangerous   small   fast   noisy

1. Mice are ______________ than orangutans.
2. Killer whales are ______________ than dolphins.
3. Cheetahs are ______________ tigers.
4. Monkeys are ______________ than snakes.

B Rewrite the following sentences using one of the comparative phrases below to fill the gaps.

much longer   much more exciting   not as intelligent

1. Giraffes have ______________ necks than llamas.
2. I think the tigers are ______________ than the penguins.
3. Koalas are ______________ as dolphins.

C Write four sentences about yourself comparing how you are now to when you were younger. For example, you could start with 'I am much taller now than I was two years ago.' When you have finished, share your paragraph with your partner.

Remember

Some two syllable adjectives can take either '–er' or 'more'.

Examples:

quiet ⟶ more quiet/quieter

noisy ⟶ more noisy/noisier

See page 152 for more on forming comparative adjectives.

Recycle, recycle, recycle

Look at these photos. Here are some items that we may have and do not need any more.

Speaking

Discuss the following questions with a partner.

1. What happens to rubbish that is not recycled?
2. Which of the items above can be recycled?
3. What do you think happens to glass, paper, cardboard, plastic and metal that is recycled?

Word builder

Use words from the box to fill the gaps in the paragraph below.

rot	resources	environment
plastic	landfill sites	conserve

Every year, more and more ____________ bottles are taken to ____________. It will take hundreds of years for them to ____________ down. One way to help the ____________ and ____________ the Earth's ____________ is to recycle as much of our waste as possible.

Speaking

Remember

When you discuss your opinions with your group, try to use some of the words from the Word builder activity.

A In groups, discuss the following questions.

1. Why do we need to reuse and recycle products? As a group, think of as many reasons as you can. Then share your ideas with the class. How many reasons has the whole class thought of? Which reason is the most popular? As a class, decide which idea is the best.
2. What is the impact on the natural landscape if we do not recycle or reuse? Discuss your opinions with your group.

B In groups, plan a new product made out of something previously used.

1. What are you going to make?
2. Does it have a purpose?
3. What are you going to make it from?
4. Present your idea to the class, making sure each person in the group has a chance to speak for between one and two minutes.

Reading corner: *Sky Hawk*

Read the extract from *Sky Hawk* by Gill Lewis and then answer the questions.

Iona has seen something that she wants to keep secret. She wants to show it to Callum.

Iona stopped at the edge of a **clearing**. A ring of large **boulders** lay in a wide circle in the sunlit space. I leaned against one and pulled some damp moss with my fingers. The pale stone underneath was bright in the spring sunshine. …

I looked up into the tree, it was an old oak that had been struck by lightning some years before … Iona kicked off her trainers and slid her fingers and toes into the tiny cracks in the **bark**. In no time, she had pulled herself up into the fork of branches above. I tried to grip the tree **trunk**, tried to wedge my feet onto the small ridges of bark, but each time my feet and hands slid. I looked up, but Iona had disappeared further up the tree … I hauled myself up into the tree and climbed higher to a natural platform of spreading **branches** … You couldn't see it from the ground. Iona had made seats from old crates and there were tins and boxes … balanced in the tree …

"I promise I won't tell anyone about this," I whispered. …

"This isn't the secret. It's better than this, a million times better." … "Open your eyes Callum," said Iona, "Look."

I still couldn't see what she was pointing at. A pile of sticks lay on the topmost branches, like driftwood stacked on a high tide.

But something was moving inside. It wasn't just a random heap of twigs and branches.

And then I saw it …

I was lost for words.

Understanding

Answer these questions.

1. Why did Iona and Callum climb the tree?
2. What season was it and what was the weather like?
3. Who climbed the tree more easily, Iona or Callum? Explain your answer.
4. Why had Iona put some old crates in the tree?
5. Callum saw a pile of sticks in the topmost branches. What do you think it was?

Glossary

bark the rough outer side of a tree

boulders large rocks

branches the parts of a tree that grow from the trunk

clearing an open space in a wood or forest

trunk the main centre stem of a tree

Writing workshop: Writing a description

You are going to plan and write a description of a secret place and something that happens there.

Planning the location

Where will your secret place be? Is it in a familiar setting, close to where you live? It might even be somewhere in your house. Or is it far away, for example in a forest? Think about these questions:

1. How did you find your secret place?
2. Why is it secret? Is something hidden there?
3. What does it look like?
4. How do you feel when you are there?

Describing your secret place

Plan which adjectives you will use to describe the secret place. Try to use powerful adjectives to create a clear picture and help the reader imagine it. Don't just describe what you can see. Try to use adjectives that describe what you can hear, smell, feel and even taste. Remember, you can also use comparative adjectives to add more detail.

Describing what happens

Now you need to decide what happens when you are in the secret place. How did it make you feel? What happened in the end?

For example:

It was silent at the house. Then I heard a footstep on the floor above. My heart beat faster and then I heard another sound. A window had been broken.

Writing, editing and proofreading

1. Now write the description of your secret place and what happened there. Write about 100–120 words.
2. When you have finished, read through your description. Have you included powerful adjectives that give a clear picture of the location? Check your spelling and correct any mistakes you have made.
3. Now share your description with a partner. Can they suggest any improvements?

Suggested reading

If you enjoyed reading the extract from *Sky Hawk*, why not try reading:

White Dolphin by Gill Lewis

The Incredible Journey by Sheila Burnford

Bug Muldoon: The Garden of Fear by Paul Shipton.

Progress check ✓

Answer the following questions.

1. Which one of the following statements is true?
   - **a** The sun is a star at the centre of the solar system.
   - **b** The sun is a planet in our solar system.
   - **c** The sun orbits Earth. (1 mark)
2. Give one example of something in our solar system that was dropped when the International Space Station was built. (1 mark)
3. List three things you might throw away each week that could be recycled. (3 marks)
4. Give one example of a countable noun and one example of an uncountable noun. (2 marks)
5. Fill the following gaps with countable nouns:
   When I go to my ____________, I like to take a ____________ and a ____________. (3 marks)
6. Choose a word from the word box to fill the gaps in the following sentences.

   plenty of | some | a large number of

   - **a** Singapore Zoo has ____________ monkeys.
   - **b** I would like ____________ information about recycling.
   - **c** We have ____________ time, so we will not be late. (3 marks)
7. What is the word 'award-winning' an example of? Use the word in a sentence of your own. (2 marks)
8. Make comparative adjectives from the following words.

   small | entertaining | cold | slow

   (4 marks)
9. Write four sentences using the comparative adjectives you made in question 8. (4 marks)
10. When planning to write a description of a place, there are things you need to think about before you start writing. Name two of these. (2 marks)

(Total: 25 marks)

Progress assessment

		😊	😐	☹️
Reading skills	I can understand the main points in a text.	O	O	O
	I can read an extended fiction text with enjoyment.	O	O	O
Use of English skills	I can use countable and uncountable nouns with words to say how many or how much.	O	O	O
	I can use compound adjectives, comparative adjectives and comparative phrases.	O	O	O
Listening skills	I can understand the main points that someone is saying.	O	O	O
	I can understand specific information in what someone is saying.	O	O	O
Speaking skills	I can give an opinion on a range of topics.	O	O	O
	I can work with my peers on classroom tasks.	O	O	O
Writing skills	I can plan and draft written work with some support.	O	O	O
	I can write, edit and proofread written work with some support.	O	O	O

✓ Action plan

Reading: I need to ______________________________

Use of English: I need to ______________________________

Listening: I need to ______________________________

Speaking: I need to ______________________________

Writing: I need to ______________________________

I would like to know more about ______________________________

2 Fit for life

Explore
- ways of keeping fit
- the importance of staying fit and healthy

Create
- a paragraph about a sporting role model
- a blog entry

Engage
- with an international footballer
- with an adventurer

Collaborate
- in discussions about different sports
- in a role play interview

In this chapter you will:

Reflect
- on the use of pronouns
- on the use the present perfect

Take care of your body. It is the only place you have to live.
Jim Rohn, author and speaker

I wanted to get really fit.
Serena Williams, tennis player

Funky and fabulous – dancing's great fun for all the family. Change 4 Life, public health programme, UK

Thinking ahead

1. How do you keep fit and healthy?
2. Which sport do you enjoy watching most? Do you have a favourite sporting personality?
3. In your free time, how often do you do physical exercise?

Word builder

Complete the following tasks.

1. Match the words on the left to the definitions on the right.

healthy	someone who is good at athletics or other sports
active	the food someone normally eats
diet	practise and learn to do something better
energy	good for you
athlete	busy and taking part in a lot of activities
train	the ability someone has to be active

2. Use the words from question 1 to complete this paragraph.

An ____________ will ____________ to improve their sporting skills, but their ____________ also needs to be ____________. The food they eat needs to give them enough ____________ to stay ____________.

Speaking

Discuss the following questions with a partner. Remember to listen to your partner's answers and ask each other questions.

1. Why is important to do plenty of physical exercise?
2. What sport or activity have you taken part in during the last week?
3. Why is it important to have a healthy diet? Do you eat healthy food?

Remember

As you discuss the questions, try to use some of the words from the Word builder activity.

The Youth Olympic Games

Read the following information on the Youth Olympic Games and then answer the questions opposite.

What is the Youth Olympic Games?

The Youth Olympic Games is a sporting event for young athletes from all over the world. It takes place every four years, with games in the summer and winter. The Summer Youth Olympics lasts for 12 days and features 28 sports. The Winter Youth Olympics lasts for 10 days and features 7 sports.

One of the main **aims** of the Youth Olympic Games is to **inspire** young people to take part in sport. The Youth Olympics also aims to bring together the world's best young athletes and educate them in the Olympic **values** of **respect**, friendship and excellence.

The Culture and Education Programme gives the athletes the chance to find out about other cultures and become ambassadors of their sport. The programme provides a range of activities, including workshops and team-building exercises.

Who takes part?

The Youth Summer Olympics is for talented young athletes aged 15–18. The Summer Youth Olympics features over 3,500 athletes while the Winter Youth Olympics features over 1,100 athletes. Not all of the participants are athletes. The non-athlete participants include young reporters.

Where and when?

The first Youth Olympics was held in the summer of 2010 in Singapore. The first Winter Youth Olympics was held in 2012, in Innsbruck, Austria.

The second Summer Youth Olympics was held in 2014, in Nanjing, China, and the second Winter Youth Olympics was held in 2016, in Lillehammer, Norway. The third Summer Youth Olympics will be held in 2018, in Buenos Aires, Argentina. The third Winter Youth Olympics will be held in 2020, in Lausanne, Switzerland.

Glossary

aims things that are intended

inspire to fill with ideas and enthusiasm

respect admiration for someone's qualities or abilities

values things that are considered important

Understanding

A Answer the following questions.

1. What does the text about the Youth Olympic Games provide for the reader? Choose the correct answer.
   - **a** information about which sports you can see at the Youth Olympic Games
   - **b** factual information about when the Youth Olympics is held and who takes part
   - **c** details about how to take part in the Youth Olympics
2. Who takes part in the Youth Olympic Games?
3. How many sports are there in the Summer Youth Olympics?
4. In which two cities were the second Youth Olympic Games held?

B Answer the following questions.

1. Find the phrase 'ambassadors of their sport' in the text. Which of the following definitions is the closest in meaning to this phrase?
   - **a** people who teach others how to play their sport
   - **b** people who represent and promote their sport in a positive way
   - **c** people who decide on the rules of a sport
2. What do you think is meant by the phrase 'non-athlete participants'?

C Complete the following short news article using words from the word box.

ambassadors	workshop	promote
medal-winning	fitness	lifestyles

Promoting healthy lifestyles

One of the aims of the Youth Olympics is to ____________ healthy lifestyles. To find out more, we went to meet Ana, one of the ____________ at the event. She explained about her role and the importance of healthy ____________ for young people. We took part in a ____________ on healthy eating and how to improve our ____________. Ana even introduced us to some of the ____________ athletes!

Pronouns

A pronoun is a word that takes the place of a noun in a sentence.

Example: Adrian and Philippe wanted to play football so **they** went to the park after school.

In the sentence above, the pronoun **they** takes the place of the nouns 'Adrian' and 'Philippe'. We use pronouns to avoid repeating nouns. This helps to make our writing more fluent.

Personal pronouns, such as **I**, **you**, **she**, **it** and **they**, usually refer to particular people or things. If we want to refer to someone or something less specifically, we can use an **indefinite pronoun**. Indefinite pronouns do not refer to a particular person or thing.

To refer to people, we can use indefinite pronouns ending in **–body** or **–one**. To refer to things, we can use indefinite pronouns ending in **–thing**.

Examples: everybody, everyone, everything
somebody, someone, something
anybody, anyone, anything
nobody, no one, nothing

Using pronouns

Remember

Personal pronouns include: I, you, he, she, it, we, they, me, him, her, us, them.

A **Fill the gaps in the following sentences with a personal pronoun.**

1. Jamal picked up the ball and threw __________ to me.
2. Nara phoned her friend Kiko and invited __________ to lunch.
3. Please can you give __________ that book?

B **Fill the gaps in the following sentences with indefinite pronouns.**

1. Does __________ have a football I could borrow?
2. I hope you have __________ you need.
3. I like watching gymnastics but I don't know __________ about it.

C **Fill the gaps in the following paragraph with pronouns.**

I had several heavy shopping bags and needed __________ to help __________ carry __________. Then one of the bags broke and __________ inside fell onto the pavement. Luckily, Sam was walking down the road and __________ helped __________ pick up the shopping and made sure __________ didn't leave __________ behind.

More indefinite pronouns

We often use **indefinite pronouns** to refer to quantities or amounts of people or things that are not precise or specific.

Examples: Please tell me **more**.
I would like **less** than that please.

Using more pronouns

A **Find the following pronouns hidden in the word search.**

many few more less much none

m	y	o	r	e	o	s
o	s	f	m	u	c	h
r	e	l	s	c	e	s
e	s	m	a	n	y	v
m	m	u	z	l	e	n
u	o	c	l	e	p	o
f	e	w	r	s	y	n
e	l	s	s	s	o	e

B **Choose indefinite pronouns from the word search to fill the gaps in the following sentences.**

1. The game was over in ____________ than an hour.
2. We took lots of photos. I only took a ____________, but you took ____________.
3. The tickets sold very quickly. There are ____________ left.
4. I thought I had lots of apples, but I don't have ____________ left.
5. I didn't eat ____________ for breakfast.

C **Choose three of the pronouns you found in the word search and use them in three sentences of your own.**

Challenge

We use **possessive pronouns** instead of nouns to talk about things that belong to someone. The possessive pronouns are: mine, ours, yours, hers, his, its, theirs.

Example: This book is mine.

Find all the pronouns in the message below and say whether they are personal, indefinite or possessive.

Hi Sara

Do you have a tennis racket I can borrow? I have been trying to find somebody who can lend me one as I have left mine at home. Suki said I could borrow hers, but then she couldn't find it.

Love Janine

Track 2.1: Sporting role models

You are going to listen to an interview with Adam Kenny, a professional football player. Adam talks about his club, what the fans mean to him and the importance of being a sporting role model. Listen to the interview and then answer the questions below.

Glossary

influences people or things that have an effect on someone

responsibility a duty or need to do something

role model someone who is an example to others

route the way taken

Understanding

A Rewrite the sentences below, filling the gaps with words from the word box.

friendship   team   relaxing   parents   fans

1. Two of Adam's biggest influences are his ____________ and his club.
2. Adam has enjoyed the ____________ and support he has received at the club.
3. Adam thinks the ____________ are important to the whole ____________.
4. He finds his journey to work ____________.

B For each question, choose the correct answer.

1. Why did Adam choose to play professional football rather than another sport?
   - **a** He didn't like any other sports.
   - **b** He was better at football than any other sport.
   - **c** His parents wanted him to play football.
2. Which of the following statements would Adam say?
   - **a** Footballers just need to score goals and it doesn't matter how they behave.
   - **b** Footballers need to behave well because they are role models and can influence young people.
   - **c** Young people are not influenced by the way footballers behave.

Writing

Complete the following tasks.

1. Think about someone who is your sporting role model. First write some notes about them. Note down their name, what they have done to be a good role model and where you first learned about them. Now add three adjectives to describe them.

   Now write a paragraph about your role model. Make sure you include the following points:

   - How have they inspired you?
   - Are you fitter now because of their influence?
   - How have they been a positive influence on you?

2. Here is a paragraph about the well-known tennis player, Novak Djokovic. However, the writer has forgotten to proofread their work. Find the eight mistakes in the spelling, punctuation and use of English. Then rewrite the paragraph correctly.

> Novak Djokovic is one of the most successful tenis players in the worlde today. They is the world number one and often beats other players easy. He was the first male player from Serbia to win a Grand Slam tennis titel He now lives in Monte Carlo withe his family

Challenge

Do you agree with Adam Kenny's view that professional footballers have a responsibility to be good role models for young people?

Do some research on the Internet to find out what other people think about this. Then write a paragraph explaining your own opinion. First state what your opinion is, and then give reasons and examples to support your views.

Interview role play

You are going to imagine you are a sporting role model and answer some questions in a role play interview with a partner. First, do some research on the Internet to find out more about your sporting role model. For example:

- Where do they train and how often do they compete?
- Who influenced them when they were young?
- What do they like best about their sport?

Now, working with a partner, pretend to be the sporting role model you have chosen and your partner is an interviewer. Answer the questions your partner asks. Then swap roles and ask your partner questions about the role model they have chosen.

The present perfect

We use the **present perfect** to refer to things that have happened **in the past**. We form the present perfect from the present tense of the verb **have** and the **past participle** of a verb.

Example: finish → has/have finished

We often use the present perfect to describe:

- something that has happened at some (indefinite) point in the past.
  Example: He has visited Italy.
- something that has happened recently that has an effect on the present.
  Example: It has stopped raining. (So it is not raining now.)
- something that started at some point in the past and is still going on in the present.
  Example: I have lived in Krakow for many years.

Using the present perfect 1

A Answer the following questions.

1. Use present perfect forms of the verbs in the word box to fill the gaps below.

search want pass

a Jake ____________ to learn how to ski for a long time.
b I ____________ everywhere but I cannot find my boots.
c Peter ____________ all of his tests.

B Change the verbs in the following sentences to the present perfect.

a I am finishing my English homework.
b I am reading a good book which I think you will like.
c Sasha is checking her messages.

C Use the past participles from the word box to complete the paragraph below.

done seen found lost put

I have ________ my phone! I don't know where I have ________ it. What have I ________ with it? Have you ________ it? Ah! I have ________ it!

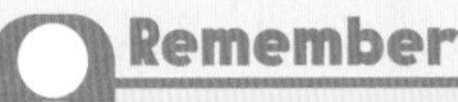

Past participles of regular verbs end in –ed. Past participles of irregular verbs end in different ways. Check in a dictionary if you are not sure. See page 155 for more.

Examples:

go → gone
be → been
take → taken
read → read

The present perfect with 'just', 'already', 'yet' and 'still'

We often use the word **just** with the present perfect when something happened a short time ago.

Example: I have just finished my book.

We use the word **already** to say something has happened early or sooner than we were expecting.

Example: I thought they would be here, but they have already left.

We use **yet** to talk about something that hasn't happened until now or something we are expecting to happen.

Example: The bus hasn't arrived yet.

We often use the word **still** with the present perfect when we are talking about something that hasn't finished, especially when we expected it to finish earlier.

Example: I still haven't finished my homework.

Using the present perfect 2

A Fill the gaps in the following sentences with 'just', 'already', 'still' or 'yet'.

1. I was expecting them to come later, but they have ______________ arrived.
2. They haven't finished playing ______________.
3. She has ______________ finished her project so she is going to relax.
4. I ______________ haven't seen that film.

B Sasha and Neiva have arranged to play tennis with Lucas and Igor. Read the conversation and fill the gaps with 'has', 'have', 'just', 'already', 'still' or 'yet'.

Sasha: Hi Neiva, I am glad you are here. ______________ Lucas and Igor ______________ arrived? Igor said they would be here before us.

Neiva: No, they haven't come ______________.

Sasha: Oh, wait. Igor ______________ sent me a message.

He says they ______________ ______________ left, so they will be a bit late.

Neiva: If they ______________ haven't arrived in five minutes, shall we start the game without them?

Keeping fit

Look at the following photographs showing different kinds of physical exercise, and then complete the activities that follow.

Speaking

In pairs, look at the photographs above and discuss the following questions.

1. What activity is taking place in each of the pictures?
2. Which of the activities involves a team and which can be done alone?
3. Which of these activities would you most like to take part in? Why?
4. Which of the activities would keep you most fit? Why?

Language for discussions

During discussions, it is important to ask for and give reasons for opinions. This will help you understand each other's ideas.

Language for asking for reasons

Why do you think that?

Why do you say that?

Why do you …?

Why do you think that is important?

Language for giving reasons

I think that because …

My reason for saying that is …

Because I …

It is important because …

Language for asking opinions

What do you think about …?

What is your view on …?

What is your opinion of …?

How do you feel about …?

Do you agree that …?

Language for giving opinions

I think that …

My view is that …

In my opinion …

I feel that …

I agree that …

Speaking

1. In small groups, discuss the following questions. Remember to give reasons for your opinions and ask each other questions to find out more.
   - **a** Do you prefer team sports or sports you can do alone? Why?
   - **b** Do you like to take risks and have adventures? Why?
   - **c** Do you prefer outdoor sports or indoor sports? Why?

2. In your groups, think about how we stay fit. Discuss the following questions:
   - **a** Do you think we learn how to stay fit when we are at school?
   - **b** Do you think people stay fit in different ways now compared with in the past?
   - **c** Do your parents keep fit in a different way from you?

Challenge

Use the Internet or books in a library to find out why exercise is good for our health. Then prepare a two-minute presentation to the class, answering the question 'Why should we keep fit?'. Include at least five facts you have found out to support your opinions. After you have given your presentation, answer any questions your classmates may have, giving more reasons for your opinions if necessary.

Reading corner: Bear Grylls' blog

Bear Grylls is well known all around the world as a writer and television presenter who has been on many exciting adventures. At the age of 23, Bear became one of the youngest people ever to succeed in climbing to the top of Mount Everest, the highest mountain in the world. In the blog below, Bear talks about where his love of adventure came from and why he loves being outdoors so much. Read the blog and then answer the questions.

Taste for adventure

I can say without a doubt that it was my dad who gave me a taste for adventure. I grew up on the Isle of Wight and have great memories of learning to climb on the sea cliffs and making **rafts** with my dad. He was **inspirational** – always told me not to be afraid ...

First adventure

The first adventure I ever had was when I was about 4 or 5, and I slept out under the stars for the first time. I had to **sneak** out without telling my mum or dad, with only my sleeping bag for **warmth** – and yes I did get in trouble the next day! But for me it was special. ...

Adventure never gets boring ...

Even now, I'm still just as excited and energetic about adventures as I was back then! It doesn't seem to matter where I am – I experience such a **feeling of belonging** when I step outside to **get my teeth into** something new! It's hard to **pin down** exactly what that is, but, at the heart of it, the outdoors is free! Your imagination can inspire the greatest adventures.

Glossary

feeling of belonging feeling at home or happy in a place

get my teeth into to become involved in with great energy

inspirational filling someone with ideas and energy

pin down to say exactly

rafts floating platforms often made from logs

sneak to move quietly and secretly

warmth the feeling of being warm

Understanding

1. How old was Bear when he had his first adventure?
2. What did Bear do on his first adventure?
3. What happened the following day?
4. Do you think Bear regrets what he did? Why?

Writing workshop: Writing a blog

You are going to write a blog entry about something that has happened to you. Blogs are web pages that are usually updated regularly and the most recent entry or 'post' appears first. People often write blogs to share their thoughts or experiences with other people. They may add a new entry each day, describing things they have been doing, including any special or important events.

To make people want to read your blog, you have to make what you write interesting. So, you need to include interesting details.

Planning your blog

Think of something interesting that has happened to you recently that you want to tell other people about. Think about the following questions:

- Where were you?
- Who were you with?
- What happened?
- What happened the next day as a result?

Suggested reading

If you enjoyed reading the blog about Bear Grylls, why not try reading his book *Mud, Sweat and Tears* or find out more about the adventurer on the website: www.beargrylls.com.

Writing, editing and proofreading

Now write your blog entry. Write about 60–80 words.

Example beginning:

It was nearly midnight so Sasha and I decided to have an exciting adventure but we knew we had to be very quiet so our parents wouldn't wake up.

Once you have written your blog, read it carefully and correct any mistakes you can find. Then swap your blog with a partner and check what they have written. Tell them what you find interesting about their blog and ways they can improve it.

Remember

In your blog, remember to include words and phrases that will make your experience sound interesting and include some of your own thoughts and opinions.

Progress check

1. Which of the following statements is true?
   a Athletes of all ages can take part in the Youth Olympic Games.
   b Athletes from all over the world take part in the Youth Olympic Games. (1 mark)

2. How many athletes take part in the Summer Youth Olympic Games?
   a over 3,500 **b** over 1,100 (1 mark)

3. Choose the correct indefinite pronoun from the box below to fill the gaps.

   someone a few anything

   a Would you like ____________ else?
   b ____________ in the gym was listening to music.
   c Only ____________ of my friends like swimming. (3 marks)

4. Fill the gaps in the following sentences with indefinite pronouns.
   a ____________ should try to stay fit and healthy.
   b I have learned a lot about Bear Grylls but I want to find out ____________. (2 marks)

5. Write two sentences of your own using indefinite pronouns. (4 marks)

6. Choose the correct present perfect form to fill the gaps.
   a I ____________ a good book which I think you will like. (am reading/have read)
   b He ____________ off his bicycle. (fell/has fallen) (2 marks)

7. Complete the sentences using the present perfect of the verbs in brackets to fill the gaps.
   a I ____________ to everything you have said. (listen)
   b Jake ____________ the piano since he was five. (play) (2 marks)

8. Write two sentences of your own using the present perfect. (4 marks)

9. Which of the following would Adam Kenny say about his fans? Choose the answer that fits best with the way you think he feels.
   a They are my role models.
   b They are always supportive and mean a lot to me.
   c They are not as important as scoring goals. (1 mark)

10. Write a short blog entry about something that has happened to you recently. Write 40–60 words. (5 marks)

(Total: 25 marks)

Progress assessment

		😊	😐	☹️
Reading skills	I can understand specific information in a text.	O	O	O
	I can recognise the attitude or opinion of a writer.	O	O	O
Use of English skills	I can use a range of pronouns including indefinite pronouns.	O	O	O
	I can use present perfect forms.	O	O	O
Listening skills	I can understand the main points that someone is saying.	O	O	O
	I can recognise what someone's opinion is when they are speaking.	O	O	O
Speaking skills	I can give an opinion on a range of topics.	O	O	O
	I can ask questions to help me understand clearly what someone means.	O	O	O
Writing skills	I can use accurate grammar in my writing.	O	O	O
	I can use the appropriate style and register in my writing.	O	O	O

✓ Action plan

Reading: I need to ______________________________

Use of English: I need to ______________________________

Listening: I need to ______________________________

Speaking: I need to ______________________________

Writing: I need to ______________________________

I would like to know more about ______________________________

3 Work around the world

Explore
- different kinds of work
- ways of travelling to work

Create
- an informal email
- a formal letter

Engage
- with a volunteer worker
- with language to persuade

Collaborate
- to plan a job advertisement
- to role play a job interview

In this chapter you will:

Reflect
- on active and passive forms
- on the use of tenses

The best preparation for good work tomorrow is to do good work today.
Elbert Hubbard, writer

Nothing will work unless you do.
Maya Angelou, writer

Choose a job you love and you will never have to work a day in your life.
Confucius, Chinese teacher

Thinking ahead

1. What job would you like to do in the future? Why do you think you would like it?
2. What sort of work do you think you would be good at? Why?
3. What kind of work do members of your family do?

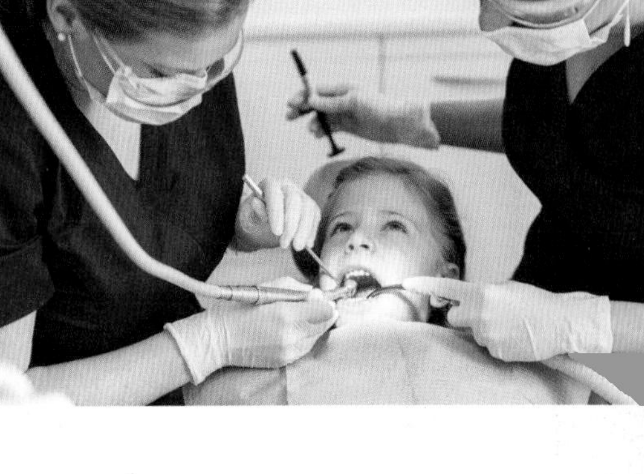

Word builder

Fill the gaps in the sentences below with words from the word box.

family business	qualifications	careers
training	team	application

1. Flavia is thinking about the different ____________ she could have when she leaves school.
2. Before Paulo started work as a teacher, he did a ____________ course.

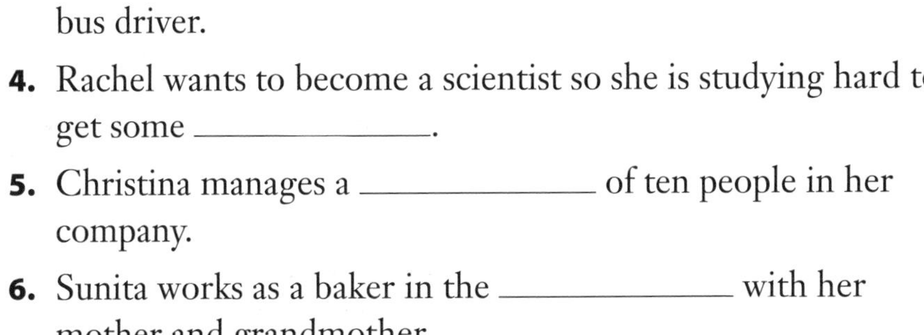

3. Ahmed has filled in an ____________ form to become a bus driver.
4. Rachel wants to become a scientist so she is studying hard to get some ____________.
5. Christina manages a ____________ of ten people in her company.
6. Sunita works as a baker in the ____________ with her mother and grandmother.

Speaking

A family business is one in which decisions are made by members of the family that own the business. Often, some or all of the employees are members of the same family. Discuss the following questions with a partner.

1. Would you like to work with your family in a family business? Why?
2. What kind of business would you like the family business to be?

Getting to work in Hong Kong

Anders is doing a school project about how people get to work in different cities around the world. He has written an email to his friend Zak, who lives in Hong Kong, asking for information for his project. Read Zak's reply and then answer the questions.

Hi Anders

Thanks for your email. I was glad to hear you're better now. Don't go climbing any more trees, will you?

Your school project sounds interesting. Yes, you're right – there are lots of ways to travel around Hong Kong. It's hard to park in the city, so many people use **public transport** to get to work rather than a car. We usually only use our car at weekends to get to places like Ocean Park (a fantastic **theme park**). You'd love it. We should go when you visit!

I don't have much experience of the buses, but I know there are buses that go into the city from every village and every part of Hong Kong. The buses are very cheap, but they can be slow and sometimes delayed. I wouldn't want to use the bus if I had to arrive on time for something.

The MTR is the fastest and most **reliable** way to travel around Hong Kong. MTR stands for 'Mass Transit Railway' and lots of people use it. I read that over 5 million trips are made on it every weekday! The MTR links Hong Kong Island to Kowloon, which is part of Hong Kong on the north side of Victoria Harbour. The trains are really fast and almost always on time. Most **commuters** who use it buy an Octopus card, so they don't have to buy a ticket every day.

Lots of people also use the Star Ferry to cross Victoria Harbour. The **ferries** leave every five to ten minutes and they're quite cheap. You get great views of the island and harbours from the ferry. And if you live close enough to where you work you can cycle or walk.

It would be great if you could visit soon! We'd all love to see you. Good luck with the project.

Cheers!

Zak

Glossary

commuters people who travel some distance to work every day

ferries boats that take people or vehicles across water

public transport buses, trains and other vehicles that can be used by everyone

reliable able to be trusted or depended on

theme park an amusement park with rides and other activities

Understanding

A Answer the following questions.

1. Which form of transport links every village in Hong Kong?
2. What is the fastest way to travel around Hong Kong?
3. What is the name of the ferry service that takes people across Victoria Harbour?

B Answer the following questions.

1. Why do many people choose to use public transport rather than a car to get to work in Hong Kong?
2. Why do so many people choose to travel on the MTR to get to work in Hong Kong? Choose the answer that fits best.
   - **a** It is cheap.
   - **b** It is fast and reliable.
   - **c** It is the only kind of transport you can get from Kowloon to the city.
   - **d** There are trains every five to ten minutes.

C Answer the following questions.

1. Eve lives in Kowloon and has an important work meeting on Hong Kong Island at 8 o'clock tomorrow morning. Which kind of public transport do you think she will choose and why?
2. If you were visiting Hong Kong as a tourist, which kind of public transport would you most like to use and why?

Challenge

In informal writing and speaking, we often use contractions to join words together. This makes our writing and speech sound more natural.

Examples: I'll (I will), can't (cannot), I'm (I am), that's (that is), I've (I have)

We use an apostrophe (') to show we missed out some letters.

Find all the contractions in Zak's email and change them into formal language by writing the words in full.

Writing

Anders has also written to you, to ask about public transport in your capital city. First, find out from the Internet or a library about the different kinds of transport in your capital city. Find out all the details you can about each kind of transport, including any special names the transport has. Now write an informal email to Anders including the information you have found out. Remember it is an informal email, so you could ask Anders how he is and wish him luck with his project. Write about 100 words.

Active and passive

When we use an **active verb**, we say **what the subject of the sentence does.**

Example: Ibrahim **switches on** his computer.

In the example above, the subject of the sentence is 'Ibrahim'. We are saying what Ibrahim does, so we use an active verb 'switches on'.

When we use a **passive verb**, we say **what happens to the subject of the sentence**. If we want to say who does the action, we use 'by'.

Example: The computer **is switched on** by Ibrahim.

In the example above, the subject of the sentence is 'The computer'. We are saying what happens to it, so we use a passive verb 'is switched on'.

To make a passive form of a verb we use the verb 'be' (am/is/are/was/were) and a past participle (the form of a verb that often ends in –ed).

Look at the following active and passive forms of the verb 'invite':

	Active	Passive
Present simple	invite/invites	am/is/are invited
Past simple	invited	was/were invited

Using active and passive forms

Remember

See pages 154–5 for more information on forming verbs with –ed, and present and past simple forms.

A Use present simple active forms of the verbs in the word box to fill the gaps in the paragraph.

ride catch make eat

Jake usually __________ his bike to work but sometimes he __________ the train. He __________ a snack before he leaves home and __________ it during the morning.

B Use present simple passive forms of the verbs in brackets to complete the following sentences.

1. The team __________ by Ted. (manage)
2. The offices __________ every Friday. (clean)
3. Lunch __________ in the canteen. (serve)

C The following sentences contain mistakes. Rewrite them, using the correct form of the past simple passive.

1. One of the office windows were broken yesterday.
2. The email sent by Ted.
3. I were invited to Ahmed's party last week.
4. Over 50 people was employed by the company.

Have something done

When we arrange for someone else to do something for us, we often say we **have something done**. Compare the following examples.

Examples: They clean the office windows every month. (They clean the windows themselves.)
They **have** the office windows **cleaned** every month. (They arrange for someone else to clean the windows.)

To use 'have something done', we use:

have/has + an object + a past participle

When we talk about having things done in the past, we use 'had' instead of 'have':

Example: They **had** the office windows cleaned.

Instead of 'have something done' or 'had something done', we sometimes say 'get something done' or 'got something done'. The meaning is the same, but 'get' is less formal than 'have'.

Examples: I **get** my hair cut every three months.
I **got** my hair cut yesterday.

Using 'have something done'

A Put the words in the correct order in the following sentences. The first one has been done for you.

1. the office furniture/delivered/had/they They had the office furniture delivered.
2. mended/had/the window/he
3. tested/has/she/her eyes/every year

B Add the correct form of 'have' or 'get' and a verb from the brackets to complete the sentences.

1. How often do you ______________ your teeth ______________ by a dentist? (check/checked/checks)
2. We ______________ the office walls ______________ last week. (paints/painting/painted)
3. My computer wasn't working properly so I ______________ it ______________. (repairing/repaired/repairs)

C Write a sentence that has a similar meaning to the following sentences. The first one has been done for you.

1. Someone mended my computer for me. I had my computer mended.
2. A professional photographer took my photo yesterday.
3. Someone put up a new fence for me last month.

Remember

When we use 'have/had something done' or 'get/got something done', the past participle always comes after the object.

Working as a volunteer

Word builder

Answer the following questions.

1. Match the words on the left to the definitions on the right.

charities	receiving money
volunteers	people who work for an organisation without being paid
communities	organisations that help people in need
paid	groups of people living in the same area

2. Use the words from question 1 to fill the gaps in the paragraph below.

Some people work in organisations such as ______________ without being ______________ for their work. These people are called ______________. The VSO (the Volunteer Service Overseas) is an organisation that arranges for volunteers to help in ______________ all around the world.

Track 3.1: Volunteering in Nepal

You are going to listen to an interview with Jonas, who joined VSO after leaving school. He spent three months as a volunteer in Nepal. Listen to what he says about his experience and then answer the questions.

Glossary

confident feeling sure you can do something

host family a family that gives someone a home for a period of time

opportunities situations that make it possible to do something

teamwork work done by a group of people working together

Understanding

A Answer the following questions.

1. How did Jonas apply to join VSO?
2. Where did Jonas live when he was in Nepal?
3. What work did Jonas do when he was there?
4. What did the volunteers use to build the bridge?

B For each question, choose the answer that fits best.

1. Why did Jonas join VSO?
   - **a** He needed a job.
   - **b** He wanted to help other people.
   - **c** He wanted to learn how to build bridges.
2. Why did the volunteers build the bridge?
   - **a** so that people could cross the river safely
   - **b** so that they could learn new skills
   - **c** because there were children living nearby
3. Why do you think VSO chose Jonas to join their team of volunteers in Nepal?
   - **a** because he had the right skills and qualifications
   - **b** because he convinced them he was the kind of person they needed
   - **c** because he wanted to go to Nepal

Challenge

Find out more on the Internet or in a library about the work of VSO or another charity. Then prepare a two-minute presentation to explain about the charity's work and what difference it makes to local communities. Then give your presentation to the class and answer any questions your classmates may have.

Speaking

Would you like to work as a volunteer? What do you think you would gain from the experience? Explain your opinions and ideas to a partner.

Writing

Jonas had to write a paragraph to explain why he wanted to become a volunteer and why VSO should choose him to go. Write your own paragraph saying why you should be chosen. Remember to try to persuade the organisation that you would make a good volunteer.

Write 40–60 words.

The present continuous

We make the **present continuous** form of a verb by using a present form of the verb 'be' (am/is/are) and a present participle (the verb form ending in –ing).

We use the present continuous to talk about actions that are happening now.

Example: I **am writing** an email.

We also use the present continuous to talk about things that are continuing over a period of time, including the present.

Example: I **am learning** English.

The present continuous can also be used for things that are planned for the future.

Example: Alisha **is flying** to Madrid next week.

To make a present continuous form in the **passive** voice, we use: am/is/are + being + past participle.

Example: My car **is being repaired** at the moment.

Using the present continuous

Remember

See pages 154–5 for more information on forming verbs with –ing and for present and past continuous forms.

A Answer the following questions.

1. Rewrite the following sentences in the present continuous.
   - a Alisha eats her lunch.
   - b Jake writes a letter.
   - c Ahmed reads a good book.
2. Use present continuous forms of the verbs in the word box to complete the sentences.

talk   make   spend

   - a Jon ______________ some time in Italy next month.
   - b The baker ______________ some bread.
   - c Mia ______________ to her mother on the phone.

B Change the following sentences into the present continuous passive. The first one has been done for you.

1. They are painting the walls. The walls are being painted.
2. They are collecting the rubbish.
3. They are knocking down the old building.

C Write four sentences of your own about things that are happening now. Use the present continuous form of verbs.

The past continuous

We make the **past continuous** form of a verb by using the past form of 'be' (was/were) with the present participle (the –ing form) of the verb.

Example: He was writing a letter.

We often use the past continuous for something that was happening at or around a particular time in the past.

Example: At 8 o'clock this morning I was walking to school.

We also use the past continuous for actions that continued for some time and were interrupted by another action.

Example: I was watching television when Alex arrived.

In the above example, notice how the past simple is used for 'arrived'.

To make a **passive** form of the past continuous, we use 'was' or 'were' with 'being' and a past participle (the verb form that often ends in '–ed').

Example: The walls were being painted.

Using the past continuous

A Rewrite these sentences using the correct form of the past continuous.

1. Rachel ______________ to some music when her telephone rang. (is listening/was listening/listened)
2. Amir ______________ blue trousers yesterday. (wore/is wearing/was wearing)
3. Max ______________ in Canada last year. (has lived/was living/is living)

B Change the following sentences into the passive form of the past continuous. The first one has been done for you.

1. Alex was carrying the bags. The bags were being carried by Alex.
2. Leni was mending the computer.
3. The teacher was preparing the lessons.
4. Jess and Felix were watching the film.

C Change the following sentences from the past simple to the past continuous active or passive.

1. I walked to school when it started to rain.
2. At 6 o'clock I rode my bike.
3. My car was repaired.

Challenge

What were you doing at 7 o'clock yesterday evening? Write three sentences using the past continuous to say what you were doing.

Talking about jobs

Working with a partner, discuss the following questions.

1. What does each of the jobs shown in the pictures below involve?
2. Which of the jobs pictured below would you most like to do and why? Discuss your reasons with your partner. Listen to your partner's choice and remember to ask questions to find out more about what they think.
3. Which of the jobs would you least like to do and why? Discuss your reasons with your partner.

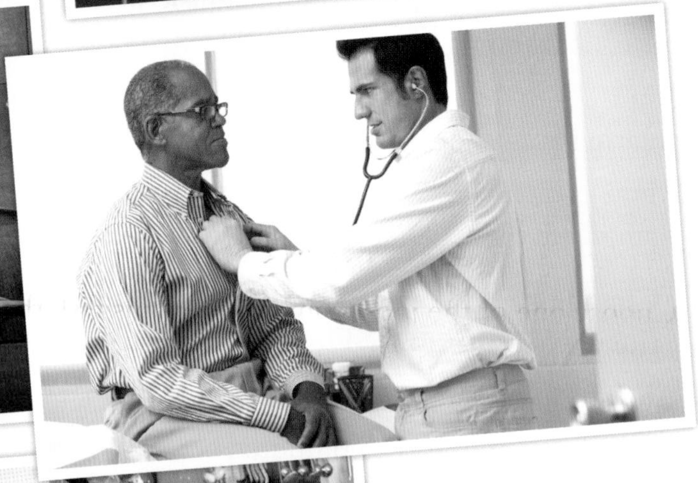

Planning a job advertisement

Work with a partner on the following tasks.

1. Imagine you work for a company or organisation that is expanding and needs to hire more people. Plan a job advertisement for someone to join your company. Think about these questions:
   - What kind of company or organisation is it?
   - What will the person be doing in the job?
   - Does the person need any qualifications to do the job?
   - What other qualities do they need?
   - How should they apply for the job?
   - Why should they join the company?
2. Once you have planned what to say, prepare a spoken advertisement for the radio or Internet. Write out the script and decide what you will say and what your partner will say. The advertisement should not be more than a minute long.
3. Next present your advertisement to the class with your partner.
4. Once everyone has presented their advertisements, vote for which job you would most like to apply for – you cannot apply for your own job!

Job interview

Work with a partner on the following tasks.

1. Choose one of the jobs from the previous task that you would like to apply for. Think about the qualities you have that would make you good at the job, as well as why you want to work for the company or organisation.
2. Now interview each other for your chosen jobs. When you are the interviewer, ask your partner why they want to do the job, what qualifications they have and what makes them suitable. When you are being interviewed, give clear answers that will persuade your partner that you are the best person for the job (you can make things up to suit the job).
3. Now tell your partner whether they have got the job or not and explain why. Give your partner some positive feedback, whether they have been given the job or not. Hopefully, you will have been successful!

Remember

Some questions just need a short answer, such as 'yes' or 'no'. Questions in job interviews often begin with a question word such as 'what', 'why' or 'when'. When you are answering questions like this, try to give as much information as you can. If you are asked what you think about something, give reasons for your opinions.

Reading corner: Job advertisements

Read the following job advertisements and then answer the questions below.

Library helper

Come and help us **shelve** our books each evening 6–8 p.m. We will **train** you and you will have the chance to take professional exams. Come to the library for an application form. The job will start next week.

Cleaner

We have an exciting opportunity for a cleaner. Come and clean our offices for two hours each day before we start work. Hours 5 a.m.–7 a.m. Start next month. Call Sam on 002233.

Farm help

We need a strong and **enthusiastic** helper to join our friendly team picking fruit from our cherry trees. Convenient hours. Come to Cherry Farm and ask to speak to Carlo – the job can start today!

Newspaper delivery

We need someone strong and fit who likes walking and is **punctual** to deliver newspapers to our customers, starting from next month. Come to Globe News on Market Street for more information. 6 a.m. start.

Vegetable cook

The Whistle and Flute restaurant needs someone to help our chef at weekends. You will be preparing vegetables at first. Full chef's training will be given for the right person. Good working conditions. 4 p.m.–9 p.m. Saturday and Sunday. Phone the restaurant and ask to speak to Sara.

Understanding

Answer the following questions.

1. Which job starts earliest in the day?
2. Which job could you start today?
3. Which jobs will give you training?
4. Which of the jobs advertised would involve working with other people?
5. Which of the jobs would you apply for and why?

Glossary

enthusiastic interested and excited

punctual arriving on time, not late

shelve put something on a shelf

train give someone skill or practice in something

Writing workshop: Writing an application letter

Imagine you have decided to apply for a role on your school council. You are going to write a letter to the head teacher to apply for the role.

Join the school council!

We need an enthusiastic, hard-working student to join us at the school council for two hours per week. To apply, write a letter to the head teacher.

Planning your letter

First plan what you are going to say in your letter. The aim of your letter is to persuade the head teacher to choose you for the role. (You can make up reasons if you do not think you would like to join the school council!)

Think about these questions:

- Why do you want to join the school council?
- Why would you be good at the role?
- Do you have any experience of doing something similar before?
- What positive words and phrases are you going to use to persuade the head teacher to choose you?

Writing your letter

An application letter needs to be more formal than a letter or email to a friend. Include your address and the date at the top of the letter. Say 'Dear Head Teacher/Ms/Mrs/Mr …' at the start of your letter.

In the first paragraph, say why you are writing the letter (you would like to apply for the role). In the second paragraph explain why you want to apply and why you would be good. To end, write 'Yours sincerely' if you have started the letter with the name of the head teacher. If you started with 'Dear Sir' or 'Dear Madam', end your letter with 'Yours faithfully'. Then sign your name below and print your name below the signature. Write about 100–150 words

Remember

In formal letters, we use a serious style of writing. We often avoid contractions such as 'it's', 'I'm' and 'you're'. It is also important to use punctuation correctly. Punctuation marks such as exclamation marks (!) are often used in informal emails and letters, but we avoid using them in formal letters.

Editing and proofreading

When you have finished your letter, check your spelling and punctuation carefully. Share what you have written with a classmate and discuss ways in which your letter might be improved.

Progress check

1. Which two kinds of public transport could you use to travel all around Hong Kong?
   a the ferry **b** the MTR **c** the bus (2 marks)

2. Write a sentence describing the Star Ferry service. (2 marks)

3. What did Jonas help to build in Nepal? (1 mark)

4. What did Jonas include on his application form to join VSO? Choose the answer that fits best.
   a details about his practical skills
   b reasons why he wanted to become a volunteer (1 mark)

5. Fill the gaps with past simple passive forms of the verbs in brackets.
   a The computer ____________ yesterday. (mend)
   b The office ____________ this morning. (clean) (2 marks)

6. Complete the following sentences with the correct form of 'have' and the verb in brackets.
   a We ____________ the windows ____________ yesterday. (clean)
   b I ____________ my hair ____________ every two months. (cut)
   c They ____________ the roof ____________ last week. (repair)
   (3 marks)

7. Fill the gaps with present continuous forms of the verbs in brackets.
   a They ____________ football. (play)
   b She ____________ for the airport this evening. (leave)
   c I ____________ an interesting book. (read) (3 marks)

8. Which two of these sentences are in the past continuous passive?
   a The meeting was being held in the manager's office.
   b The teacher was talking to the class.
   c The computer was being mended. (2 marks)

9. Think of three things you should include in a job advertisement.
   (3 marks)

10. Write a short job advertisement for someone to come and work in a restaurant. (6 marks)

(Total: 25 marks)

Progress assessment

		🙂	😐	🙁
Reading skills	I can understand the reasons given for ideas in a text.	O	O	O
	I can work out the meaning in a text from the context.	O	O	O
	I can find out information from a range of reference resources.	O	O	O
Use of English skills	I can use active and passive forms and 'have/get done'.	O	O	O
	I can use present continuous and past continuous forms.	O	O	O
Listening skills	I can understand the detail of what someone is saying.	O	O	O
	I can understand the meaning of what someone is saying, even if it is not stated directly.	O	O	O
Speaking skills	I can work with my peers on classroom tasks.	O	O	O
	I can link my comments to what others say.	O	O	O
Writing skills	I can develop arguments, supported by reasons and examples.	O	O	O
	I can use formal and informal styles in my writing.	O	O	O

✓ Action plan

Reading: I need to ______________________________

Use of English: I need to ______________________________

Listening: I need to ______________________________

Speaking: I need to ______________________________

Writing: I need to ______________________________

I would like to know more about ______________________________

4 Leisure

In this chapter you will:

Explore
- how we spend our leisure time
- how people celebrate special days

Create
- a message to a friend
- a short playscript

Engage
- with an actor
- with an author

Collaborate
- to share our opinions
- in discussions about leisure time

Reflect
- on the use of adverbs
- on the use of comparatives

Reading a book is like rewriting it for yourself. Angela Carter, author

Love is playing every game as if it's your last. Michael Jordan, basketball player

Adventure is worthwhile. Aesop, story teller

Thinking ahead

1. Do you prefer to spend your leisure time at home or doing activities outside?
2. Do you think you have enough leisure time? Would you like to have more?
3. What do you like to do when you are not at school?

Word builder

Look at the sign below for a new club at the leisure centre. Fill in the gaps with the correct words from the word box.

sport   films   cinema   spare   choose   exciting

Join our new club!

Would you like to spend your __________ time doing __________ activities?

We play __________ and go to the __________ to watch the latest __________.

You can __________ to do whatever you wish.

We're open every day 4.00p.m. until 6.00p.m.

Apply online or see us here for more information.

Speaking

1. With a partner, talk about what you do in your free time. Do you like reading? Sports? Seeing friends?
2. Which leisure activities do you think are the most popular for young people of your age? Discuss your opinions with your partner. See how many words you can use from the Word builder.

Star Chat: *Into the Woods*

Many people enjoy going to the cinema to watch films in their leisure time. Read the online interview about the musical film *Into the Woods*, which was inspired by stories such as 'Cinderella' and 'Jack and the Beanstalk'. We meet the actor Daniel Huttlestone, who plays the character of Jack. Daniel talks about what it was like to work with a large cow called 'Milky White'.

National Geographic Kids [NGK]: Hi Daniel! What was it like working with such a big animal as Milky White? Our animal expert thinks cows are scarier than sharks – were you frightened at all? Was he a pain?

Daniel Huttlestone [DH]: I had a great time working with the cows! … I wasn't scared of them. You would think that cows are cute but trust me, working with one is a whole different experience. Sometimes she had good days, sometimes not! …

NGK: … The film is full of big stars. Who was your favourite person to work with and why, and did you get star struck?

DH: Everyone was amazing to work with. I spent most of my time with Lilla (who plays Red Riding Hood), James (who plays the Baker) and Billy (who plays Rapunzel's Prince). Of course I got a bit star struck when I met the big stars – anyone would!

NGK: The term "I wish" **features heavily** throughout the film. If you could wish for anything right now, what would it be?

DH: Well, I'd love to continue to work on such great film projects for the rest of my life. If I had to pick **a wish** though, it would be to train with the Chelsea football team. That would be great!

NGK: We agree, it would! So do you like spending time outdoors … or are you more of a city boy?

DH: I love the outdoors! I like the city as well, but I'm really into sports like football and tennis, so I'm always outside!

NGK: Thanks for answering our questions, Daniel!

Glossary

features heavily happens often

a wish something you would like to happen, but is unlikely or impossible

Understanding

A Answer the following questions.

1. What does the interview on page 58 provide for the reader? Choose the correct answer.
   - **a** information about the plot of the film *Into the Woods*
   - **b** the opinions and thoughts of one of the actors in the film
2. What does Daniel like to do in his leisure time?

B Answer the following questions.

1. Which of the following sentences would Daniel say?
   - **a** The cows were cute and always easy to work with.
   - **b** It wasn't always easy to work with the cows but I enjoyed it.
2. What does Daniel want to do in the future? Choose the correct answer.
   - **a** continue with his acting career
   - **b** become a footballer

C Daniel says he was 'a bit star struck' when he met the famous stars in the film. Explain in your own words what you think he means.

Remember

If you do not understand the meaning of a word or phrase you read, you may be able to guess its meaning from the words around it.

Speaking

You are going to describe to a partner a book that you have recently read or a film that you have recently seen. Think about what you liked and what you didn't like. Now think of ways of making what you say interesting. Then, take turns to describe your book or film. Can you think of interesting questions to ask your partner to find out more information?

Writing

Write a message to a friend asking if they would like to see a film with you. Include the following in your message.

✓ What film will you see and which day will you see it?

✓ What time does the film start and how will you get to the cinema?

Write 40–60 words.

Adverbs

We often use adverbs to give more information about a verb. Adverbs can tell us how, when, where or how often something happens or happened.

Examples: **How:** The sun shone **brightly**.
When: She saw the film **today**.
Where: She left the book **here**.
How often: She **always** reads before she goes to sleep.

Many adverbs are made from adjectives + –ly.

Example: careful → carefully

Some adverbs are irregular, which means they do not follow the rules.

Example: good → well

Some adverbs have the same form as the adjective.

Examples: hard, fast, late, early, daily

Using adverbs

Remember

If an adjective ends in a 'y', change the 'y' to an 'i' before adding '–ly' (lazy → lazily). See page 153 for more information on forming adverbs.

A Are the following adverbs telling you how, when, where or how often?

1. tonight/tomorrow/yesterday
2. happily/calmly/loudly
3. never/sometimes/rarely
4. there/nearby/outdoors

B Make adverbs from the following adjectives and then use them to fill the gaps in the sentences below.

late easy quiet early

1. I climbed the stairs __________ because my sister was asleep.
2. I finished the puzzle __________.
3. We arrived __________, so we missed the beginning of the film.
4. I don't want to be late. I would rather arrive __________.

C Use 'how often' adverbs of your own to fill the gaps in the following sentences.

1. I __________ walk to school.
2. I __________ eat healthy food.
3. I __________ go to the cinema on Friday evening.

Comparatives

We use **comparative adverbs** when we want to compare the way two things are done or the way two things happen. See page 153 for more information on forming comparatives.

With adverbs that end in '–ly', we usually use the word 'more' before the adverb to make a comparative adverb.

Example: quietly → **more** quietly

With short adverbs that do not end in '–ly', we usually add '-er'.

Example: hard → harder

Some adverbs have irregular comparative forms.

Examples: well → better badly → worse

We often use the word 'than' when we are making a comparison in a sentence.

Example: Amir was listening **more carefully than** Michael.

To make comparisons, we can also use adverbs with phrases such as **as ... as**, **far less ...** and **not as ... as**.

Examples: Let's walk **as quickly as** possible. I asked him to speak **far less loudly**.

Using comparatives

A Choose the correct form of the comparative adverb to complete each sentence below.

1. You weren't feeling well yesterday. Are you feeling ______________ today? (more well/better)
2. Please will you drive ______________. (slower/more slowly)
3. He was working ______________ than ever before. (more hard/harder)

B Use comparative phrases from the box below to complete the following sentences.

just as far less far more

1. You will need to run ______________ quickly if you want to win the race.
2. Leila can jump ______________ high as Alisha.
3. I finished the puzzle ______________ easily this time.

C Look at the pictures in the margin. Write three sentences that compare one way of travelling with another. Try to use comparative adverbs and comparative phrases.

Track 4.1: Interview with Jacqueline Wilson

You are going to listen to an interview with the children's author Jacqueline Wilson (actors are playing the parts). Jacqueline Wilson has won many awards for her books. Before you listen, work with a partner to predict some of the questions the interviewer may ask. Then listen carefully to the interview and answer the following questions.

Understanding

A For each question, choose the correct answer.

1. When did Jacqueline Wilson start to write stories?
   - **a** when she was 22
   - **b** when she was a child
   - **c** when she was 17
2. Where did Jacqueline Wilson have the idea for Tracy Beaker's surname?
   - **a** in the bath
   - **b** at school
   - **c** in a dream
3. How long does Jacqueline Wilson say it takes children to read her books?
   - **a** too long
   - **b** three days
   - **c** six months
4. How long does it take Jacqueline Wilson to write a book?
   - **a** three days
   - **b** up to six months
   - **c** a year

Glossary

corrections changes made to put mistakes right

distorted giving a false idea

evolved developed slowly

feisty lively and brave

formal strictly following the rules

inspire fill someone with ideas and enthusiasm

published printed and sold

thrilled to bits very happy

B **For each letter in brackets, choose the correct word from the list below.**

> **Interviewer:** How did you first become interested in **(a)** ________? Did any author or **(b)** ________ inspire you?
>
> **Jacqueline Wilson:** I loved **(c)** ________, I liked pictures, and it evolved from there. No, at my primary school, they made a fuss of me, I was chosen to read my **(d)** ________ aloud. At secondary school, stories were made to be more formal, so I had lots of **(e)** ________.

a	reading	writing	drawing
b	friend	a parent	teacher
c	writing	books	school
d	books	stories	essays
e	mistakes	corrections	awards

C **Answer the following questions.**

1. Which of the following statements would Jacqueline Wilson say about her book *The Illustrated Mum*.
   - **a** It is a sad story but it is possibly my favourite of all the books I have written.
   - **b** I prefer *Tracy Beaker*.
2. Which of the following sentences best describes how Jacqueline Wilson feels about the TV series 'Tracy Beaker'.
   - **a** She is delighted with it.
   - **b** She isn't happy with it because she didn't write the scripts.

Challenge

Listen to Track 4.1 again and then answer the following questions.

1. Write a sentence explaining what you think Jacqueline Wilson means when she says each of the following sentences.
   - **a** 'At secondary school stories were made to be more formal'
   - **b** 'Do it the school way at school and your own way at home'.
2. What do you think Jacqueline Wilson means when she says 'Each time I start a book, I want it to be this and that and it hardly ever does'?

Writing

Write a set of three questions you would like to ask the author of your favourite book. When you have finished, share your questions with a partner. Has your partner thought of different questions?

Adverbs in sentences

When we use an adverb in a sentence, it often comes after the verb.

Example: They chatted **quietly**.

When a verb has an object, we usually put the adverb after the object.

Example: He opened the door **slowly**.

Adverbs that tell us when something happens often come at the end of a sentence.

Example: I will see my friends **tomorrow**.

Adverbs that tell us how often something happens usually come before the verb. When the verb is 'to be', the adverb usually comes after the verb.

Examples: I **usually** read before I go to sleep. She is **always** happy.

If we want to emphasise (give importance to) an adverb, we sometimes put it at the beginning of the sentence.

Examples: **Suddenly**, I woke up. **Sometimes**, I catch the bus to school.

Using adverbs in sentences

A For each pair of sentences, choose the one that has the adverb in the right position.

1. He read quickly the book./He read the book quickly.
2. He was loudly speaking./He was speaking loudly.
3. I often play tennis on Fridays./I play tennis on Fridays often.

B Answer the following questions.

1. Correct the following sentences by putting the adverb in the right position.
   - **a** Did you see last night the film?
   - **b** He well plays the piano.
   - **c** They listen usually to music in the evening.
2. Rewrite the following sentences, adding the adverb in the correct position.
   - **a** I go to the cinema with my friend. (often)
   - **b** The football team are playing. (well)
   - **c** He listened. (carefully)

C Write four sentences using the following adverbs.

fast never tonight happily

Too, also and either

The words 'too', 'also' and 'either' are adverbs. We use them like other adverbs, to give more information about a verb.

We use the word 'too' after a positive verb. It usually comes at the end of a sentence or clause.

Example: I enjoyed reading the book. My brother enjoyed it too.

We also use 'also' with a positive verb. 'Also' usually comes before the verb, unless the verb is 'to be'.

Examples: My favourite book is *The Illustrated Mum*. My brother **also** likes it.
I like reading books in my spare time. My brother **is also** keen on reading.

In negative sentences, we use the word 'either' instead of 'also' or 'too' to give the idea of agreement.

Example: I didn't enjoy the film. My friend didn't like it either.

Using too, also and either

A Read the following conversation between two friends, Leyla and Alisha. For each number, insert the words 'too', 'also' or 'either'.

Leyla: I thought the film was really good. I am so glad you could come **(1)** __________. Did you enjoy it?

Alisha: Yes. I thought it was very funny and it **(2)** __________ made me cry! What did you think about the ending?

Leyla: I didn't want the film to end, but the ending made me feel extremely happy. Did you feel like that **(3)** __________?

Alisha: I didn't want the film to end **(4)** __________! But I was **(5)** __________ pleased it had a happy ending.

B Answer these questions.

1. Change the following sentences from negative to positive.

a Anna hasn't seen the film and Rahini hasn't seen it either.

b Ali doesn't want to go swimming and Emir doesn't want to go either.

2. Change the following sentences from positive to negative.

a Jake is studying hard for his exams and Carol is also working hard.

b Lian is very good at dancing and Jo is also a good dancer.

Challenge

As well as giving more information about verbs, adverbs are sometimes used to modify (change slightly), or give more information about, adjectives.

Examples: I was **so** tired.

The book is **very** long.

Find all the adverbs that are used to modify adjectives in activity A. Then use the adverbs in sentences of your own to modify some other interesting adjectives.

New places and special days

Look at the pictures of people enjoying their leisure time. What do you like to do in your spare time?

Speaking

Many people use their leisure time to visit new places. Some people visit places in their own country and some people visit other countries. Everybody has a different opinion about what makes a good place to visit.

With a partner, take turns to talk about the following questions. Listen to your partner's opinions and remember to ask questions about what they are saying.

1. What places have you visited? What other places would you like to visit and why?
2. Is it important to go to new places? Can we learn new things from travelling?

Word builder

Match the words and phrases on the left with the correct meanings on the right.

anniversary	a party or special event to show something is important
public holiday	a large meal for lots of people
celebration	to go somewhere new
feast	a journey from one place to another
expedition	a day when most people in a country do not have to go to work
take a trip	a day when you remember something special that happened on the same date
transport	vehicles used to get from one place to another

Speaking

Talk with a partner about what the people in the pictures below could do on their special days. Try to use words from the Word builder above.

Remember

When you are talking about things that might or could happen, you can use modal verbs like **can/could**, **will/would**, **shall/should**, **may/might** and **must/ought**.

Anita and Alex Rossi are about to celebrate a special anniversary. They have been married for 50 years!

Karim and Husna are deciding how to celebrate their birthdays this year.

Sophia and Antonis are planning what to do on the next public holiday.

Reading corner: *The Lion, the Witch and the Wardrobe*

Read the following extract from *The Lion, the Witch and the Wardrobe* by C.S. Lewis. A group of children have entered a whole new world where it is always winter. In this extract, Edmund notices that the season is changing. C.S. Lewis writes using lots of description, allowing us to imagine ourselves there too.

Every moment more and more of the trees shook off their **robes** of snow. Soon, wherever you looked, instead of white shapes you saw the dark green of **firs** ... delicious **sunlight** struck down on to the forest floor and **overhead** you could see a blue sky between the tree tops ...

Soon there were more wonderful things happening. Coming suddenly round a corner into a **glade** of silver birch trees Edmund saw the ground covered in all directions with little yellow flowers ... The noise of water grew louder. **Presently** they actually crossed a stream ... Only five minutes later he noticed a dozen **crocuses** growing round the foot of an old tree – gold and purple and white ...

A bird suddenly **chirped** from the branch of a tree ... And then there was chattering and chirruping in every direction, and then a moment of full song, and within five minutes the whole wood was ringing with birds' music, and wherever Edmund's eyes turned he saw birds ...

Understanding

Answer the following questions.

1. What did Edmund notice as he walked through the wood? Choose the correct answer.
   - **a** that it was getting colder
   - **b** that there were more and more trees
   - **c** that it was changing from winter to spring
2. What was the first thing Edmund noticed that made him think the season was changing?
   - **a** white shapes
   - **b** less snow on the trees
   - **c** flowers
3. What sounds did Edmund hear as he walked through the wood?
4. Which colours did Edmund notice in the woods?

Glossary

chirped made a small, sharp bird sound

crocuses small spring flowers

firs evergreen trees with leaves like needles

glade an open space in a wood or forest

overhead above, high up

presently soon

robes long, loose pieces of clothing

sunlight the light from the sun

Writing workshop: Writing a playscript

You are going to write a short playscript in which Edmund tells his sister Lucy about his walk through the woods.

Planning your playscript

Edmund is full of excitement and wants to tell Lucy about what he has seen. Before you write your playscript, think of words and phrases you can use to describe:

✓ why Edmund was so excited

✓ what he saw and heard

✓ how he felt.

Plan your playscript with the following features:

✓ the speakers' names written on the left before the words that are spoken

✓ any directions or instructions to the actors written in brackets before the words that are spoken.

Remember

When you are writing your playscript, try to use comparative adverbs or comparative phrases, such as 'far less … than' or 'not as … as'. You can also use phrases such as 'slightly … than', 'a bit … than', 'much … than' and 'a lot … than'.

Writing, editing and proofreading

You can begin your playscript like this. Think of words you can use to fill the gaps.

Edmund: (excitedly) Lucy, guess what has happened to me?

Lucy: (__________) I would love to know! Why are you so __________?

Now continue writing the playscript. Try to add as much description as possible about what Edmund has seen. Write 100–120 words.

When you have finished your playscript, read it through carefully and correct any mistakes. Then show it to a partner. How are your playscripts different? How can they be improved?

Progress check ✓

Answer the following questions.

1. What does the actor Daniel Huttlestone do in his spare time? (1 mark)

2. Which one of the following statements would Daniel Huttlestone say?

a I want to give up acting and become a footballer.

b I would love to train with the Chelsea football team. (1 mark)

3. How many books has Jacqueline Wilson written? Choose the correct answer.

a 22 **b** over 80 **c** 50 (1 mark)

4. What would Jacqueline Wilson say about where her ideas come from? Choose the correct answer.

a I don't know exactly where my ideas come from.

b I get my ideas from dreams. (1 mark)

5. Make the following adverbs into comparative adverbs.

easily often well late

(4 marks)

6. Write four sentences using the comparative adverbs you made in question 5. (4 marks)

7. Rewrite the following sentences, putting the adverbs in brackets in the right positions.

a I saw the film. (yesterday)

b I have time to watch TV. (rarely) (2 marks)

8. Write two sentences using the comparative adverb phrases 'far less …' and 'much more …'. (2 marks)

9. Use the word 'too', 'either' or 'also' to fill each of the gaps.

I love swimming and my brother loves to swim ________. I ________ love tennis. I am not very fast at running and my brother isn't ________. (3 marks)

10. Write three sentences about what you like to do in your spare time. Try to make your sentences interesting and use some comparative adverbs. (6 marks)

(Total: 25 marks)

Progress assessment

		🙂	😐	🙁
Reading skills	I can understand the meaning in a text, even if it is not stated directly.	O	O	O
	I can work out the meaning in a text from the context.	O	O	O
Use of English skills	I can use comparative adverbs and comparative phrases.	O	O	O
	I can use adverbs in the correct position in sentences, including 'too', 'either' and 'also'.	O	O	O
Listening skills	I can understand specific information in what someone is saying.	O	O	O
	I can work out the meaning of what someone is saying from the context.	O	O	O
Speaking skills	In a discussion, I can use words and phrases that relate to the topic I am studying.	O	O	O
	I can ask questions to help me understand clearly what someone means.	O	O	O
Writing skills	I can write, edit and proofread written work with some support.	O	O	O
	I can use the appropriate layout for a playscript.	O	O	O

✓ Action plan

Reading: I need to ______________________________

Use of English: I need to ______________________________

Listening: I need to ______________________________

Speaking: I need to ______________________________

Writing: I need to ______________________________

I would like to know more about ______________________________

5 Friends

In this chapter you will:

Explore
- friendship
- shared interests among friends

Create
- a letter to a friend
- a description of what makes someone a good friend

Engage
- with old friends who meet again
- with two penfriends

Collaborate
- to talk about how to be a good friend
- to role play a meeting between friends

Reflect
- on abstract nouns
- on noun phrases

A friend in need is a friend indeed.
Proverb

There is nothing on this earth more prized than true friendship.
Thomas Aquinas, scholar

The only way to have a friend is to be one.
Ralph Waldo Emerson, writer

Thinking ahead

1. Spend some time thinking of all the words and phrases the term 'friend' brings to mind.
2. Write down as many as you can in two minutes.
3. Compare your list with that of your neighbour. How similar were your lists?

Word builder

Use words from the word box to complete the sentences below.

rely	supports	shared
trust	listen	laugh

1. My best friend always ______________ me.
2. I can ______________ on my best friend and talk to her about my problems.
3. I joke with my friends and they make me ______________.
4. I know I can ______________ my friends because they always tell me the truth.
5. I have lots of ______________ interests with my friends.

Remember

As you discuss your opinions, try to use words and phrases from the 'Thinking ahead' and 'Word builder' activities.

Speaking

In pairs, discuss the following questions.

1. What is a friend?
2. When does someone you see often – a classmate perhaps – become a friend?
3. Do you make friends easily? How?

What makes a good friend?

Michele and Andreas are good friends. Read the emails they have sent each other then answer the questions opposite.

Tomorrow
Michele
Sent: **Wednesday, September 2016 6:32pm**
To: **'Andreas'**
Cc:

Hi Andreas

I'm sorry but I have to cancel our fishing trip tomorrow afternoon. It's such a shame because I always look forward to our trips – they are always good fun.

My little brother has a hospital appointment at 3p.m. tomorrow. Mum is taking him and she says I should go with them. She thinks my brother will feel happier if I'm there. I told Mum I'd arranged to go fishing with you but she said you would understand. I am sure you know how disappointed I am.

How about Friday afternoon, same time, same place? Let me know.

Michele

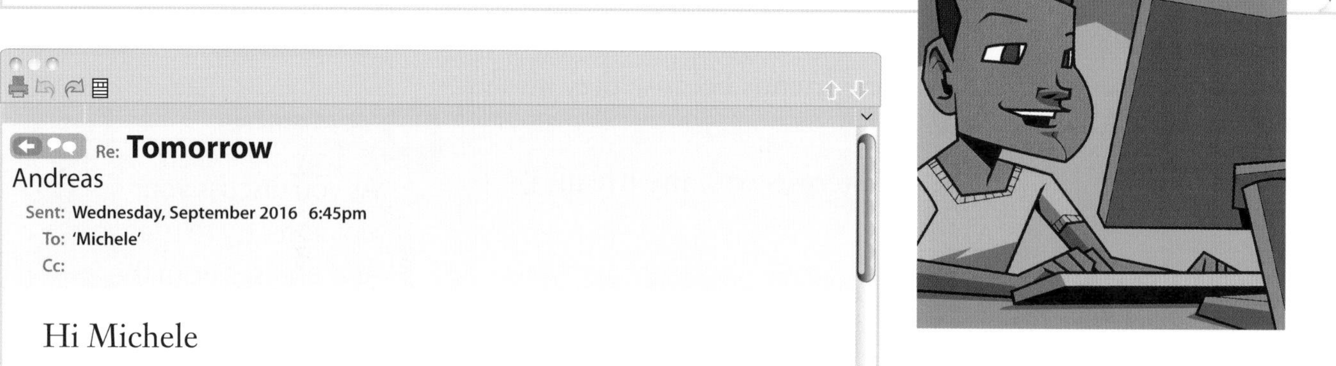

Re: **Tomorrow**
Andreas
Sent: **Wednesday, September 2016 6:45pm**
To: **'Michele'**
Cc:

Hi Michele

I'm really sorry that you can't come tomorrow, but of course I understand. The good news is that Friday afternoon is fine, but can we meet a bit later – about 3p.m.? Friday's not long to wait and it'll be just as much fun.

Good luck at the hospital tomorrow. I know your brother has been quite ill. It must be hard for you too. I'm sure it'll be easier for your brother if you are there. Just make sure you don't tell him any of your awful jokes! I hope it all goes well.

See you on Friday.

Andreas

Understanding

A For each question, choose the correct answer.

1. Why is Michele emailing Andreas?
   - **a** to say how much he enjoys going fishing with him
   - **b** to tell him he can no longer meet him tomorrow
   - **c** to complain about having to go to the hospital
2. Why is Michele no longer free?
   - **a** He has a hospital appointment.
   - **b** He has to take his mother to hospital.
   - **c** He has to go with his little brother to hospital.

B For each question, choose the correct answer.

1. How is Michele feeling?
   - **a** disappointed that he can't go fishing
   - **b** annoyed with his brother
   - **c** very worried that Andreas won't understand
2. When Michele replies, what must he let Andreas know?
   - **a** how the hospital appointment went
   - **b** whether he can meet him at 3p.m. on Friday
   - **c** whether his brother is feeling better

C What words in the emails tell us that Michele and Andreas are good friends? Write down all you can find in the emails.

Writing

Think again about what Andreas says in his email to support his friend Michele. Now write a short paragraph of 40–60 words about what you think makes someone a good friend. Remember to use some of the vocabulary you have just learned.

Nouns

Compound nouns are made when two or more words are combined to make a new word.

Example: foot + ball = football

Compound nouns can be written as:

- **one word,** such as classmate, newspaper
- **two words,** such as human being, swimming pool, tennis court
- **two or more hyphenated words,** such as check-in, sister-in-law.

Some nouns are **concrete nouns**. Concrete nouns name things we can see, smell, taste, hear or touch.

Examples: friend, flower, lemon, sound, skin

Some nouns are called **abstract nouns**. They name things that we cannot see, smell, taste, hear or touch. They refer to thoughts, feelings, ideas and character.

Examples: honesty, trust, love, loyalty, kindness

Using compound nouns

A **Make three compound nouns from the words in the box below.**

stop clip ball bus paper basket

B **Use the words you made in A to fill the gaps in the following sentences.**

1. I am going to play ________ with my friend.
2. We waited at the ________ for 30 minutes.
3. Please can you pass me a ________?

Using concrete and abstract nouns

A **Make two lists with the headings 'Concrete' and 'Abstract'. Then put the following words in the correct list.**

computer	friendship	information
friend	kindness	library

B **Write three sentences of your own using the abstract nouns from A.**

C **Write a short paragraph about a friend, using four abstract nouns. Write 40–60 words.**

–ing forms used as nouns

We often use the **–ing** form of verbs as **nouns**.

Example: I enjoy **singing**. ('Singing' is used as a noun – it is the thing I enjoy.)

The –ing form of a verb can be the **subject** of a verb.

Example: **Swimming** is fun.

The –ing form of a verb can also be the **object** of a verb.

Example: My friend Lucas loves **reading**.

Using –ing forms as nouns

A Make –ing forms of the verbs below. Then use the words to complete the following sentences.

fish read meet learn play

1. I enjoyed __________ you.
2. We are looking forward to __________ tennis.
3. __________ books is relaxing.
4. Michele and Andreas like __________ in the lake.
5. __________ a new language takes time.

B Add you own –ing words to fill the gaps in the following sentences.

1. I am looking forward to __________ you.
2. __________ is good for you.
3. My friends all love __________ music.

C In which two of the following sentences are the –ing forms used as nouns?

1. She is swimming in the lake.
2. I have just read an interesting book.
3. She enjoys walking.
4. Have you finished reading the book I lent you?

Remember

The subject of a verb is the person, place or thing that is doing or being something. The object of a verb is the thing or person that is affected by the verb.

Example:

Lucas ate the ice cream.

In the example above, 'Lucas' is the subject and 'the ice cream' is the object.

Track 5.1: Old friends meet again

You are going to listen to a conversation between Marianna and Lucia. They were close friends when they were at school, but they lost contact and have not seen each other for 60 years. Before you listen, discuss with a partner what you think they might talk about and complete the Word builder activity below.

Word builder

Match the words on the left to their definitions on the right.

twins	in a foreign country, across the sea
inseparable	back together after being apart
overseas	path leading to something
reunited	two children born at the same time from the same mother
trail	always together

Understanding

A Listen carefully to Track 5.1 and for each question select the answer that fits best.

1. Where did Lucia work as a nurse?

a America **b** Australia

2. Why did some people call Lucia and Marianna twins?

a They looked alike.

b They always sat next to each other at school.

c They had the same birthday.

3. Which 'twin' is the older?

a Marianna **b** Lucia

4. Where did Marianna go to look for Lucia?

a their old school **b** the old library

B **Listen again to the conversation between Marianna and Lucia and then answer these questions.**

1. Why was Marianna unable to contact Lucia when she got married?
2. What happened to Marianna and Lucia during the years they were apart? Write a sentence about each of them.

C **What do you think the two girls looked like when they were at school? Write a brief description based on what they say. Write about 40 words.**

Speaking

In pairs, you are going to act out the reunion of Lucia and Marianna.

First you need to prepare. You can use these words to begin:

Lucia:	Who is it? Do I know you?
Marianna:	Lucia, it's Marianna. Do you remember?
Lucia:	Who? ... Who?
Marianna:	Marianna – the 'Terrible Twin'!
Lucia:	Oh! Oh, is it really you, Marianna?
Marianna:	Yes, dear Lucia! It's me. Do you remember those days?
Lucia:	Of course, it's coming back, all the fun we had … How did you find me?

Now you continue. What memories will the friends share – of school and their time together? Think of an incident involving the 'Terrible Twins' that they can talk about. For example:

- missing school one afternoon to go for a walk
- hiding in a school cupboard and being locked in.

What other people will they recall? For example:

- their teacher
- other children.

Challenge

Find out from an older person, in your family perhaps, what friends they had when they were schoolchildren. Ask them:

- Do they still keep in touch?
- Are there some they no longer have contact with?
- What happened to them?
- What did they do together?

Now write a short report about what you have found out.

Noun phrases

A **noun phrase** is a phrase, or group of words, that contains a noun and other words that tell us more about the noun.

Noun phrases often begin with words such as 'the', 'a' or 'an', 'that', 'my', 'some', 'both (of)', 'half (of)' and 'all (of)'. Words like this are called 'determiners'. Noun phrases may also include adjectives and other words that give even more information about the noun. Look at the following sentences. The noun phrases are in bold.

Examples: **My friend** has sent **an email**.
My best friend has sent **a long email**.
My best friend has sent **a long, funny email**.

Noun phrases help us to put more information into our writing and make it more interesting.

Using noun phrases

A Answer the following questions.

1. Choose words from the word box to complete the noun phrases in the sentences below.

that   my   your

a Do you know ____________ brother?
b I will come to ____________ house after school.
c Please could you pass me ____________ blue pen?

2. Write out the three noun phrases you made in question 1.

B Choose words from the box below to fill the gaps in the following sentences. You do not have to use all of the words in the box, and sometimes you will need more than one.

a	warm coat	both of	half of	all of
the	apple	my	friends	some

1. I wanted to meet up with ____________ after school.
2. It's cold outside. You will need to wear ____________.
3. I have only eaten ____________.

C Make noun phrases using the following abstract nouns. Include a determiner and an adjective in each noun phrase.

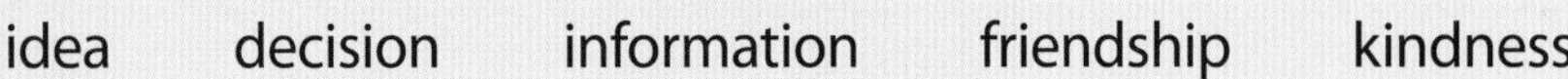

idea   decision   information   friendship   kindness

More noun phrases

As we have seen, noun phrases often include adjectives that come before the noun. They may also include words after the noun that give even more information about the noun.

Example: **My best friend who lives in Germany** has sent **a long, funny email about her day at school.**

Noun phrases can be the subject or the object of a verb. In the sentence above, the subject of the verb 'has sent' is the noun phrase 'My best friend who lives in Germany'. The object of the verb is the noun phrase 'a long, funny email about her day at school'.

Using more noun phrases

A Write out all the noun phrases from the following sentences.

1. She wanted to join the tennis club that had just started up at school.
2. I have just finished reading a really interesting book, which my friend lent me.
3. She couldn't find the blue shirt that she was given for her birthday.

B Answer the following questions.

1. Make interesting noun phrases using the words in the word box. Include words that come before and after each noun.

bread house car film

2. Use the noun phrases you have made in four sentences of your own.

C Answer the following questions.

1. Read the message on the right, which Michele has sent to Andreas. Can you find four noun phrases in his message?
2. Michele must have forgotten to check his text message for mistakes. There are no commas, full stops or capital letters and there are some spelling mistakes. Rewrite his text message, correcting the mistakes.

Friends together

Our friends are often those who share our interests and do the things we like doing. Look at the photos. Which are you most like?

Speaking

With a partner, look at the photos above and discuss the following questions.

1. What are the people doing in each of the pictures?
2. What words could you use to describe the people in the pictures.

Word builder

Match the words on the left to their definitions on the right.

adventurous	timid and afraid to meet and talk to other people
confident	interested in music
musical	not nervous or afraid
shy	keen to do exciting, bold things

Making friends

In pairs, discuss the following questions.

1. What kind of person do you think you are? Are you like one of those pictured opposite, a mixture or something different? Begin by asking each other some questions. For example:
   - Do you like the outdoors?
   - Do you like to spend a lot of time reading?
   - Are you musical? What sort of music do you like?
   - Are you sporty? What sports do you like playing or watching?
   - Do you like to think quietly about events?
   - Do you make friends easily?
2. A new student has joined your class. How can he or she be made welcome and how will you become friends with the newcomer? Talk about these questions:
   - What things might you talk about?
   - What could you do together?
   - Where might you take them?
3. Act out the meeting with the new student, taking it in turns to be the new student. Before you act it out, think about:
   - Where the meeting will take place
   - Who will speak first
   - What you will do if the new student is shy, or speaks only a few words of your language.

Remember

When you are talking, try to use some of the words from the Word builder activity above.

Reading corner: Letter to a friend

Myra and Anika have never met, but they have got to know each other well by writing letters to each other. Read Myra's letter to Anika and then answer the questions.

Dear Anika,

I enjoy being your **penfriend** so much! I can't wait until you get your Internet and we can email and even speak online. But until then letters will be fine.

A lot has been happening at school recently. We have a new classmate! He's called Leon and he has just moved here from Germany with his family. He's really nice. He's coming round to my house on Saturday with his sister Anna. Joe is coming, too. He's in my brother's class.

The other exciting thing that has happened is that a new tennis club has started up after school on Thursdays. I know how much you love tennis! I joined the club and have been playing with Kiara every week – I think I'm getting better, but I'm sure I'm not as good as you!

How are things with you? I hope your mother is feeling better now and you're enjoying school. Do you like your new teacher? Write back soon!

With love from

Myra

Understanding

For each question, choose the correct answer.

1. Who has just joined Myra's class at school?

a Anna **b** Joe **c** Leon

2. What is happening on Saturday?

a Myra is playing tennis with Kiara.

b Leon and Anna are going to Myra's house.

c Kiara and Leon are going to Myra's house.

3. What do you think Anika said in her last letter to Myra?

a that she had joined a new tennis club

b that her mother was ill and she had a new teacher

c that she had just got a computer with Internet

Glossary

penfriend someone in another country you write to, usually without meeting them

Writing workshop: Writing an informal letter

You are going to plan and write an informal letter to a penfriend telling them about something that has happened at school.

Plan your letter

Before you write your letter, there are some things you need to think about.

Your penfriend

It will help for you to have a picture in your mind of your penfriend. Think of some real-life friends you have. What kind of things would you tell each other about? Give your friend a name. Think about these questions:

- What does your friend look like?
- How did you start writing to each other?
- Have you ever met?
- What interests do you share?

Vocabulary and style

Make use of some of the vocabulary you have learned in this unit, as well as some abstract nouns and noun phrases. Keep the style of your letter informal, using friendly, chatty language.

What has happened?

What are you going to tell your penfriend about? It doesn't have to be something dramatic, just something you would mention to a friend. For example, you could tell them about:

- a visitor talking to your class
- an accident – perhaps someone dropping and breaking something
- a new student arriving in your class.

Were you excited or frightened? What will you tell your friend?

Writing, editing and proofreading

Write your letter, about 200 words. Then check your spelling, punctuation, grammar and vocabulary. Share what you have written with a classmate. Discuss ways in which your letter might be improved.

Suggested reading

In *The Diary of a Young Girl*, the young Dutch girl Anne Frank writes letters to an imaginary penfriend to tell of her experiences in hiding with her family in war time.

Progress check 

1. Fill the gaps in the sentences with words from the word box.

supports listens rely

a My best friend is someone I can ___________ on.
b My friend ___________ to me when I talk about my problems.
c He always sticks up for me and ___________ me. (3 marks)

2. Why did Michele email Andreas? Choose the best answer.
a to tell him he couldn't go fishing tomorrow
b to tell him his brother was ill (1 mark)

3. When does Michele suggest they meet?
a same time but on Friday
b 3 p.m. on Friday (1 mark)

4. Choose the correct form of the following compound nouns.

a	birth-day	birth day	birthday
b	washing machine	washingmachine	washing-machine
c	passer-by	passerby	passer by (3 marks)

5. Which of the following nouns are abstract nouns?

happiness ice peace health honesty email

(3 marks)

6. What is the name of Marianna's husband?
a Franco b Alex c She is not married. (1 mark)

7. What did Lucia do when she was in America? (1 mark)

8. Which one of these sentences uses an –ing verb as a noun?
a Walking is good for your health.
b I was swimming when you called me. (1 mark)

9. Write out the noun phrases from the following sentences.
a I like playing tennis with my friends.
b I have just seen my old friend Jenny who moved to France.
c That bread that you have just baked smells delicious. (6 marks)

10. Write a short email to a friend to arrange a tennis game. (5 marks)

(Total: 25 marks)

Progress assessment

		🙂	😐	🙁
Reading skills	I can recognise the features of informal emails and letters.	O	O	O
	I can recognise the attitude or opinion of a writer.	O	O	O
Use of English skills	I can use compound nouns, abstract nouns, -ing forms as nouns and noun phrases.	O	O	O
	I can use a range of determiners.	O	O	O
Listening skills	I can understand the detail of what someone is saying.	O	O	O
	I can understand extended accounts of events.	O	O	O
Speaking skills	I can link my comments to what others say.	O	O	O
	In a discussion, I can use words and phrases that relate to the topic I am studying.	O	O	O
Writing skills	I can use the appropriate style and register in my writing.	O	O	O
	I can use punctuation accurately in my writing.	O	O	O
	I can spell words accurately in my writing.	O	O	O

✓ Action plan

Reading: I need to ______________________________

Use of English: I need to ______________________________

Listening: I need to ______________________________

Speaking: I need to ______________________________

Writing: I need to ______________________________

I would like to know more about ______________________________

6 Where we learn

In this chapter you will:

Explore
- where and how we learn
- remote schooling

Create
- a newspaper article
- different forms of questions

Engage
- with School of the Air
- with how we learn new things

Collaborate
- to discuss learning new skills
- to role-play an interview

Reflect
- on modal verbs
- on conjunctions

> **Any fool can know. The point is to understand.**
> Albert Einstein, scientist

> **Tell me and I forget, teach me and I may remember, involve me and I learn.**
> Benjamin Franklin, American statesman

> **We learn from failure, not from success!**
> Bram Stoker, author

Thinking ahead

1. There is a saying 'The world is our classroom.' What do you think this means?
2. What kinds of things do you learn outside school?
3. When we are learning something new, do we always need a teacher?

Word builder

Use words from the word box to fill the gaps in the following paragraph.

understand	information	learning
Internet	reading	skill

_____________ does not just take place in school. As young children at home, we learn the _____________ of speaking by copying sounds made by our parents. As we grow older, we increase our knowledge through ____________, conversations, travelling and other activities. At school, teachers give us valuable _____________ about different topics and help us to _____________ it. Nowadays, we often use computers and the ____________ to help us learn.

Speaking

In a small group, discuss the following questions.

1. How do computers and the Internet help us learn?
2. Is there a difference between finding out information and understanding it?
3. What are the best ways of learning and where are the best places to learn?

School of the Air

Read the information below about School of the Air and then answer the questions that follow.

School of the Air: the world's largest classroom!

Australia is a huge country, with many **isolated** areas, a long way from towns and cities. Some children live hundreds of kilometres away from their nearest neighbours, and even further away from the nearest school. How do these children learn and get an education? For many children, the answer is 'School of the Air'.

School of the Air is a form of **remote schooling** that has been operating in Australia since 1951. By 2005, School of the Air had more than 16 schools around Australia, covering a huge area of over 1.5 million square kilometres.

How does it work?

Students using School of the Air have their lessons at home. Until 2009, teachers and students **communicated** using special two-way radios. Nowadays, School of the Air lessons are given using Internet and **satellite** technology.

School of the Air teaches the same subjects as other schools in Australia. Most students spend about one hour a day receiving lessons from a teacher. Then they work on projects and **assignments** which the teacher has set.

The teachers try to visit each student at least once a year. Each school also organises camps and other events, when students can spend time with their classmates.

New technology

New technology has brought many changes to School of the Air. Teachers often give their lessons in front of a video camera so the students can see and hear them. The students can also speak to the teacher, and take part in group discussions with other students, who may be over 1,500 kilometres away.

Glossary

assignments pieces of school work

communicated spoke to each other

isolated far away from towns and cities

remote schooling a way of being educated without being present at a school

satellite a spacecraft used to send and receive information

Understanding

A For each question, choose the correct answer.

1. What does the 'School of the Air' text provide for the reader?
   - **a** opinions about the best way to educate children who cannot get to school
   - **b** information about how to find out about School of the Air
   - **c** factual information about how some children in Australia are educated
2. What is School of the Air?
   - **a** a way of educating students without the need for teachers
   - **b** a system of schooling that educates students from a distance
   - **c** home schooling by parents using the Internet
3. When were the first lessons given by School of the Air?
   - **a** 2009 **b** 1951 **c** 2005

B Answer the following questions.

1. Why do you think the title describes School of the Air as 'the world's biggest classroom'?
2. In what way is School of the Air similar to other schools in Australia?
3. Describe two ways in which School of the Air is different from other schools.

C Read the following summary of the information about School of the Air. Find four pieces of information that are different from the information you read on page 90.

> School of the Air was set up in the 1950s to provide an education for children in remote areas. Today, the students use special two-way radios to speak to their teachers. School of the Air teaches different subjects from other schools in Australia. The students spend three hours a day having lessons with the teacher.

Challenge

Students who study at School of the Air use computers so that they can have their lessons at home. Write two paragraphs about the advantages and disadvantages of learning from home using a computer. Then write a short conclusion saying whether you would like to have your lessons at home.

Modal verbs

Modal verbs are a special group of verbs. We use them before other verbs to show an opinion or attitude, for example about how possible we think something is.

The modal verbs are: can, could, may, might, will, would, shall, should, must, ought (to)

We can use modal verbs to show:

- that something is **possible** or somebody **is able to** do something;

  Examples: He **can** visit you tomorrow.
  He said he **couldn't** visit you.
  Ibrahim **can** speak English very well.

- **how sure** we are about something or **how certain** it is.

  Examples: I **may** see you tomorrow. (I am not sure.)
  It **might** rain tomorrow. (It is not certain.)
  I **will** phone you this afternoon. (I am sure.)
  I told her I **would** see her later. (I was sure.)

Using modal verbs

A Use words from the box to complete the following sentences.

can't
could
can
couldn't

1. Sandro ________ play the trumpet very well.
2. I am afraid I ________ come to the concert.
3. He was speaking so quietly, I ________ hear him.
4. Felix ________ understand everything I was saying.

B Add words from the box to complete Neiva's message.

can might will would

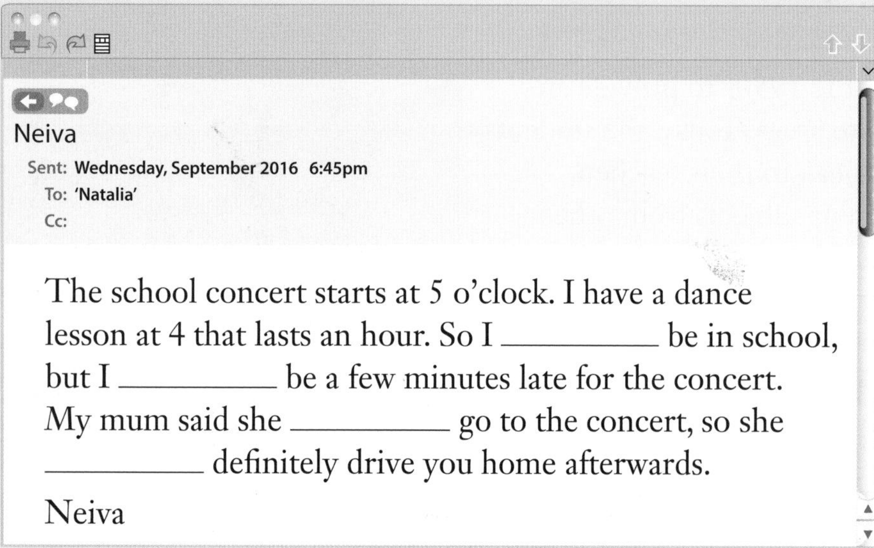
Neiva
Sent: Wednesday, September 2016 6:45pm
To: 'Natalia'
Cc:

The school concert starts at 5 o'clock. I have a dance lesson at 4 that lasts an hour. So I ________ be in school, but I ________ be a few minutes late for the concert. My mum said she ________ go to the concert, so she ________ definitely drive you home afterwards.

Neiva

Remember

Modal verbs cannot be used on their own. They are always followed by a main verb. The form of a modal verb always stays the same – we cannot add 's', '-ed' or '-ing'.

More modals

We use the modal verbs 'should' and 'ought to' to give **advice**.

Examples: It is cold outside, so you **should** put your coat on.
It's a really good book, so you **ought to** read it.

To make **suggestions**, we often use 'could'.

Example: We **could** see the film at the weekend.

We use 'must' to talk about something that is **necessary** or **has to be done** (something that is obligatory). We use 'mustn't' to tell someone not to do something.

Examples: We **must** leave straight away.
You **mustn't** make too much noise.

To give someone **permission** to do something or to say that something is allowed, we use 'can' or 'may'.

Examples: Yes, you **can** go outside.
Students **may** leave early today.

Using more modals

A Use a modal verb from the box below to complete the following sentences.

should ought to could

1. You __________ visit him tomorrow if you have time.
2. You have to get up early, so you __________ go to bed soon.
3. It is raining so you __________ take an umbrella.

B Fill in the gaps in the school rules with modal verbs.

School Rules

1. School uniform __________ be worn at all times.
2. You __________ run in the corridors.
3. Students __________ keep library books for up to two weeks.
4. If you have any problems you __________ speak to your teacher.

C For each question, write an answer using a modal verb.

1. What shall we do this weekend?
2. When can I come and see you?
3. I am feeling unwell. What do you think I should do?

Track 6.1: School of the Air

You will hear an interview with Christina, who lives in a very remote part of Australia and attends School of the Air. Listen carefully to the interview and answer the questions.

Understanding

A Answer the following questions.

1. How far does Christina live from the nearest school?
   - **a** over 30 kilometres
   - **b** over 400 kilometres
   - **c** over 300 kilometres
2. Why does Christina attend School of the Air? Choose the answer that fits best.
   - **a** because her parents want her to
   - **b** because she lives too far away to travel to an ordinary school
   - **c** because she wants to make friends
3. What kind of technology does Christina use when she is having her lessons?
   - **a** a radio and a computer
   - **b** a radio
   - **c** a computer

B For each question, choose the correct answer.

1. What does Christina like best about School of the Air?
   - **a** going to camp
   - **b** having lessons at the same as other students and getting to know them
   - **c** being taught the same things as students who go to ordinary schools
2. What does Christina find annoying about School of the Air?
   - **a** that she sometimes misses lessons if the Internet isn't working
   - **b** that she never sees her classmates
   - **c** that she has too many lessons each day

Glossary

cattle cows on a farm

count on one another to trust each other

community all the people who live in a place

remote a long way from other people

satellite dish a large dish-shaped aerial which receives television signals

Track 6.2: School of the Air

You are now going to listen to the second part of the interview with Christina. Listen carefully and answer the questions.

Understanding

A Answer the following questions.

1. How far does Christina live from her nearest neighbours? Choose the correct answer.

   a 200 kilometres **b** an hour away **c** 300 kilometres

2. What time does School of the Air begin for Christina each day?

a 

b 

c 

B For each question, choose the answer that fits best.

1. Which of the following statements would Christina say?
   - **a** We are always busy but I love my life here.
   - **b** I would prefer to live in the town.
2. How would you describe the language used by the interviewer?
   - **a** friendly and quite formal
   - **b** friendly and very informal
3. Which one of these questions is a closed question?
   - **a** Do you have any brothers or sisters?
   - **b** When are you able to see your neighbours?
   - **c** What is your typical day like for you?

Remember

Closed questions can be answered 'yes' or 'no'.

Example:

Do you attend School of the Air?

Open questions cannot be answered with just 'yes' or 'no'.

Example:

Why do you attend School of the Air?

We often use **open questions** to find out more information and to ask for an opinion.

Speaking

Think of two questions that you would like to ask someone who attends School of the Air. Then, with a partner, take turns to be an interviewer and the student. When you are the interviewer, keep the style of your language quite formal. Remember to listen carefully to your partner's answers. Try to build on what they say and ask other questions. When you are the student, answer all the questions your partner asks, including those you may not be expecting.

Questions and requests

Some questions require a specific answer, such as 'yes' or 'no'. To form a question like this, we put the subject after the 'auxiliary' (helping) part of the verb (words such as 'is', 'has' or 'have' that come before the main verb).

Examples: **Is she** using the computer? **Has the lesson** finished?

In the **present simple**, we use **do** or **does** before the subject. We use 'do' with 'I', 'we', 'you' and 'they'. We use 'does' with 'he', 'she' and 'it'. In the past simple, we use **did**.

Examples: **Does he** want to eat his lunch? **Did they** enjoy the film?

We often use modal verbs in questions and requests.

Examples: **Can** I ride my horse?
Could you take me home?
Will you show me how to do that?
May I borrow your book?
Would you like to go to camp?

Using questions and requests

A Put the words in the correct order to make questions. Remember to add a capital letter and a question mark.

1. was hungry she
2. you do music listening to like
3. I glass another have may of water
4. you would to after like play school basketball

B Change the following statements into questions or requests. The first one has been done for you.

1. You can ride a bike. Can you ride a bike?
2. He likes playing tennis.
3. She worked hard at school.
4. She is eating her lunch.
5. He can have another apple.

C Write three questions of your own, beginning with the words shown.

1. Why __________?
2. Can __________?
3. Did __________?

Remember

Open questions often begin with a question word such as 'what', 'where', 'which', 'who', 'when', 'why' or 'how'. To form these questions, we add the question word to the start of the question.

Examples:

When does he want to eat his lunch?

Why are you doing that?

Reasons and explanations

When we are answering open questions, such as 'Why do you think …?' or 'What makes you say …', we often need to give **reasons** for our opinion or an **explanation** of something.

When we explain a reason, we can use the **conjunctions** 'because', 'as' and 'since'.

Examples: She likes going to camp **because** she can see her friends.
As she was feeling hungry, she had lunch early.
Since she had some free time, she decided to ride her horse.

We sometimes shorten 'because' to 'cos' in informal speaking.

When we are talking about reasons and results, we can also use 'so … that' and 'such a … that'.

Examples: It was **so hot that** we stayed inside.
It was **such a hot day that** we stayed inside.

Using reasons and explanations

A Fill the gaps in the following sentences with a conjunction.

1. She missed her lesson __________ the Internet wasn't working.
2. __________ it was so hot, she opened the window.
3. She went outside, __________ she had finished her work.

B Make one sentence from each set of two sentences using 'because', 'as' or 'since'.

1. She couldn't do her homework. She had missed the lesson.
2. She went to bed early. She was very tired.
3. She had got up early. She had time to feed the animals.

C Complete the following sentences using 'such … that' or 'so … that'.

1. The farm is __________ far away from the nearest school __________ Christina can't go to an ordinary school.
2. She has been __________ busy with her school work __________ she hasn't had time to ride her horse.
3. It was __________ nice weather __________ they were able to have their meal outside.

Remember

A conjunction is a word that we use to join parts of a sentence together.

Examples: but, and, or, so, although, because, since, as.

Sometimes, we use conjunctions such as 'since' and 'as' at the beginning of a sentence.

Learning new skills

We learn new things every day. Some of the skills we learn take a lot of practice. Look at the pictures of people learning new things.

Speaking

In a small group, discuss the following questions.

1. What skill is being learned in each of the pictures above?
2. Do we always need other people to help us learn new skills?
3. Do you enjoy learning things that take practice? Why or why not?

Word builder

Use the words in the word box to fill the gaps in the paragraph below.

mistakes	play	practise	
properly	observing	repeat	copying

When we are very young, we learn many things through ______________. We also learn by ______________ and ______________ what other people are doing. When we learn a new skill, we often have to ______________ before we know how to do it ______________. We can learn from our ______________, but may have to ______________ actions many times before we can do them well.

Speaking

A In a small group, discuss the following questions.

1. What new things have you learned by copying or observing someone else?
2. What skills have you learned through trying and making mistakes?
3. What new skills have you been taught by someone else?
4. What can you do now that you couldn't do a year ago? How did you learn this skill?

B With a partner, complete the following task.

Think of a skill that you have. It may be a skill you learned a long time ago or it may be something you have started to learn recently. Now, working with a partner, take turns to tell your partner about the skill and how you learned it (or how you are learning it). Did you find it easy to learn or did you have to practise it (or are you still practising)? Answer any questions your partner may have, including ones you may not be expecting. Swap roles when you have finished.

Remember

During your discussions, remember to listen to what the other members of your group are saying and ask questions to show you are listening. If you want a specific answer, ask a closed question (such as 'Are you having lessons?'). If you want someone to share their ideas about something, ask an open question (such as 'How did you learn how to do this?').

Reading corner: Healthy breakfasts

Read the newspaper article below and then answer the questions that follow.

A healthy breakfast: the secret to success at school?

- **Eating breakfast can help you learn**
- **Students who eat a healthy breakfast do better in tests**

Many **studies** around the world have shown that students who eat breakfast are able to concentrate better than those who don't. But can eating breakfast help you do better in tests and does it matter what you eat?

To find the answers to these questions, scientists have carried out a new study. In 2015, 5,000 students aged nine to eleven at over 100 schools took part in the study. The scientists looked at what the students ate for breakfast and the scores they achieved in school tests.

Hannah Littlecott, who led the study, said that the results gave the "strongest **evidence** yet of **links** between what pupils eat and how well they do at school."

The results of the study suggested that students who ate a healthy breakfast every day were almost twice as likely to achieve an **above-average** score in school tests than those who didn't.

In the study, a healthy breakfast was made up of fruit, dairy, bread and/or cereals such as oatmeal. Unhealthy breakfasts, made up of crisps or high-sugar items, were not linked to higher grades.

So choosing the right foods for breakfast may really help our brains!

Understanding

1. Why did the scientists carry out the study described in the article?
2. When did the study take place?
3. How many schools took part in the study?
4. Why did the scientists look at the students' test scores?
5. What did the results of the study suggest?

Glossary

above-average better than the usual standard

evidence information and facts that give people a reason to believe something

links connections between two things

studies detailed investigations

Writing workshop: Writing a newspaper article

Many scientists believe that certain foods help us learn more effectively and can help our brains function better. You are going to write a newspaper article about foods that are said to be good for the brain.

Planning your article

First, do some research on the Internet to find out which foods are said to be good for the brain. Decide which foods you are going to mention in your article. Then try to find some reasons why these foods are thought to be good for the brain.

Remember

When you have finished writing your newspaper article, remember to check it carefully for mistakes in spelling or punctuation.

Try to include the following features in your article:

- a headline that grabs the reader's attention
- bullet points giving a summary of the main points of the report
- an introduction
- short paragraphs, with clear information about which foods are good for the brain and why
- a reference to what someone has said
- a conclusion.

Writing, editing and proofreading

Now write your article. Try to include the features listed above.

The following paragraph from a newspaper article has not been proofread. Proofread it and correct the mistakes in spelling, grammar and punctuation. (See if you can find all ten mistakes.)

> a new study has found than oatmeal is one off the most healthy foods you can to eat four breakfast oatmeal contains protein and carbohydrates that given us energy slowly and keeps our minds working well throughout the day

Challenge

'All children should eat breakfast before they go to school.' Do you agree?

Write three short paragraphs. In the first, explain your own opinion. In the second paragraph, give another point of view, with reasons why you do not agree with that opinion. Finally, write a short conclusion, giving a summary of your ideas.

Progress check

1. Why was School of the Air set up? Choose the correct answer.
   - **a** so that students in remote areas of Australia could make friends
   - **b** to provide an education for children living in remote areas of Australia (1 mark)
2. How often do School of the Air teachers visit their students?
   a every day **b** at least once a year **c** never (1 mark)
3. Why does Christina get up so early in the morning?
   - **a** to help her family feed the animals on the farm
   - **b** so she can ride her horse before her lessons start (1 mark)
4. Which of these statements would Christina say?
   - **a** I am lucky to attend School of the Air.
   - **b** I wish I could go to an ordinary school. (1 mark)
5. Fill the gaps with a modal verb.
   - **a** It is very late, so you ____________ go to bed.
   - **b** Of course you ____________ borrow my phone. (2 marks)
6. Write four questions using the modal verbs from the word box.

can	may	will	could

   (4 marks)
7. Fill the gaps in the following paragraph.
   It was ____________ cold outside ____________ I stayed indoors. ____________ Tina had a warm coat, she went for a walk. (3 marks)
8. Rewrite the following sentence, correcting the five mistakes in grammar, punctuation and spelling.
   The studi found that a healtthy breakfast is can make a diference to how well we learn (5 marks)
9. Newspaper articles often include headlines. Describe one other feature you might find in a newspaper article. (1 mark)
10. Write a headline and three bullet points for a newspaper article on School of the Air. (6 marks)

(Total: 25 marks)

Progress assessment

		😊	😐	☹
Reading skills	I can read a range of extended non-fiction texts.	O	O	O
	I can understand inconsistencies in short texts.	O	O	O
Use of English skills	I can use a range of questions and modal forms for different purposes.	O	O	O
	I can use the conjunctions 'since' and 'as', and the structures 'so … that' and 'such a … that' in explanations.	O	O	O
Listening skills	I can recognise what someone's opinion is when they are speaking.	O	O	O
	I can recognise the features of interviews and how formal and informal language is used in different situations.	O	O	O
Speaking skills	I can use formal and informal language when I speak.	O	O	O
	I can respond to unexpected comments.	O	O	O
Writing skills	I can develop arguments, supported by reasons and examples.	O	O	O
	I can use the appropriate layout for a newspaper article.	O	O	O

✓ Action plan

Reading: I need to ______________________________

Use of English: I need to ______________________________

Listening: I need to ______________________________

Speaking: I need to ______________________________

Writing: I need to ______________________________

I would like to know more about ______________________________

7 Culture and customs

In this chapter you will:

Explore
- birthday customs
- traditional celebrations

Create
- a paragraph about a birthday celebration
- a poem

Engage
- with different customs
- with Chinese New Year

Collaborate
- in discussions about celebrations
- in a performance of a poem

Reflect
- on the use of prepositions
- on conditional sentences

We are all different. Different customs, different foods, different langugages ... but not so different that we cannot get along with one another.
J. Martin Cohe, author

Ritual is important to us as human beings. It ties us to our traditions and our histories.
Miller Williams, American poet

Customs form us all.
Aaron Hill, playwright

Thinking ahead

1. What festivals and celebrations do you have in your country? What sort of things happen on those days?
2. Do you take part in any traditional customs or celebrations? Which is your favourite and why?
3. Do people in your country or region sometimes wear traditional clothes?

Challenge

Read the quotations on page 104. If you are unsure of the meaning of any of the words, check their definitions in a dictionary. Then write three sentences explaining in your own words what you think each quotation means.

Word builder

Use the words in the word box to complete Luisa's email to Mara.

festival firework crowds dancing birthday party

The festival
Luisa
Sent: Wednesday, October 2016 2:45pm
To: 'Mara'
Cc:

Hi Mara

I hope you enjoyed your ________! If only we lived nearer to each other, I could have come to your ________. At the weekend, we went to a ________ in the city. There was lots of music and people were ________. The ________ were huge! At the end, there was a big ________ display. If you came next year, I am sure you would love it!

Speak soon!
Love Luisa

Speaking

How do you celebrate birthdays in your family? In pairs, discuss the following questions.

1. What happened on your last birthday?
2. What did you enjoy about it?
3. What is your ideal birthday celebration?

Birthday celebrations around the world

People celebrate birthdays in many different ways around the world. Read the information below about different birthday customs and then answer the questions that follow.

Australia
Many Australian children celebrate their birthdays by eating 'fairy bread', which is buttered bread covered with coloured **decorations** made from sugar known as 'hundreds and thousands'.

Germany
On their birthdays, German children take **treats** to school for their classmates.

Candles are lit for children to show their age, one for each year and a special 'life' candle is lit every year until the child reaches the age of 12.

Hungary
In parts of Hungary, birthday guests take part in a **ritual** in which they pull the ears of the birthday boy or girl while singing 'Happy birthday and may you live till your ears reach your ankles.'

India
Many children in India are given new clothes on their birthday. A party is held in the afternoon when special food is served. Presents are given wrapped in brightly coloured paper, as plain paper is thought to bring bad luck.

Jamaica
Traditional celebrations in many parts of the Caribbean, especially Jamaica, include throwing flour at the person whose birthday it is. The idea is to make them look older!

Mexico
In Mexico, an important part of a birthday celebration is the piñata. Piñatas are brightly coloured containers made from clay or **papier mâché**. They are filled with sweets and other small treats and hung from the ceiling or the branch of a tree. Party goers hit the piñata with a stick to break it open and enjoy what is inside.

Vietnam
Traditionally, birthdays are not usually celebrated in Vietnam. Everyone becomes a year older on the first day of the New Year in Vietnam, or 'tet'. So birthday celebrations for everyone are part of the new year festivities.

Glossary

decorations things that make something look more attractive

papier mâché a mixture of paper and glue used to make models or ornaments

ritual a regular ceremony

treats small gifts such as sweets

Understanding

A Answer the following questions.

1. What do children take to school on their birthdays in Germany?
2. In which country might you have your ears pulled on your birthday?
3. When do people in Vietnam celebrate their birthdays?

B Answer the following questions.

1. How are Jamaicans made to look older on their birthdays?
2. Why in India do people not wrap birthday presents in plain paper?
3. Why do children at parties in Mexico hit piñatas with sticks?

C Write two sentences giving instructions for how to make 'fairy bread'.

Challenge

Use the Internet or books in a library to find out about other birthday customs around the world. Then prepare a presentation to give to a small group. Remember to explain what happens in each country you talk about and say what is unusual about it. At the end of your presentation, be ready to answer questions from the group.

Writing

Complete the following tasks.

1. Fill the gaps in Sara's email to Marta with words of your own.

Party invitation
Sara
Sent: **Wednesday, October 2016 2:45pm**
To: **'Marta'**
Cc:

Hi Marta

I hope you're well! My brother will be ____________ years old tomorrow! Today, I helped my mum bake a ____________ for him. We will give him his ____________ tomorrow, but his ____________ is on Saturday. We have bought lots of colourful ____________ to put up around the house. If you are free, we would like you to come, too. It's at ____________ o'clock at our house. I hope you can make it!

Love Sara

2. Now write an invitation of your own, asking a friend to come to a birthday celebration. Don't forget to say where the party is and when.

Prepositions

A **preposition** is a word or phrase that shows the relationship between nouns, pronouns and other words in a sentence.

Examples: on, in, under, by, to, of, without, in front of, ahead of, apart from, close to, out of

Prepositions are often used:

- with time words: I am leaving **at** six o'clock.
- to show where something or someone is: She is sitting **next** to me.
- to show movement or direction: I am walking **down** the hill.
- to say how we do something: We are going **by** car.

A **prepositional phrase** is formed using a preposition followed by a noun, pronoun or noun phrase.

Examples: below ground, after you, during the last month

Using prepositions

A **Use the prepositions on the left with the words and phrases on the right to make prepositional phrases.**

after	the birthday party
outside	the bed
under	the new building
over	the garden fence

B **Choose three of the prepositional phrases you made in A and use them in three sentences of your own.**

C **Complete the following message using prepositions from the word box.**

up	on	with	next to	close to
out of	to	on	after	

Hi Marta

I'm glad you can come ________ my brother's party! I forgot to tell you where our house is! It is quite ________ the park. Go ________ the hill on the way ________ town, and ________ about 100 metres you will see a house ________ a red door ________ a big tree. I hope you can find it! See you ________ Saturday!

Love Sara

More prepositions

We often use prepositions after adjectives.

Examples: Italy is **famous for** its food.
Max is **good at** English.
The teacher was **pleased with** the class.

The preposition 'like' means 'similar to', 'the same as' or 'in the same way as'.

Examples: She looks **like her mother**.
It's spring, but it feels **like winter**.

The preposition **as** means 'in the form of' or 'in the position of'. We use it to talk about the job or function of someone or something.

Examples: She worked **as a teacher** for six years.
They chose Leon **as captain** of the football team.

Using more prepositions

A Complete the sentences below using prepositions from the word box.

of   on   about

1. You should be very proud ______________ yourself.
2. Max is very keen ______________ football.
3. I am excited ______________ your birthday.

B Use the prepositions 'as' or 'like' to complete the sentences.

1. I love hot, sunny weather ______________ this.
2. I wouldn't pick this film ______________ my first choice.
3. It's not ______________ you to arrive late!

C Complete this message from Sara's brother to Marta, filling in the gaps with prepositions from the word box.

of   on   to   at   with

Hi Marta
It was great to see you _______ my party _______ Saturday.
I am really pleased _______ the computer game you gave me.
It was very kind _______ you to give it _______ me.
Joe

Chinese New Year

You are going to listen to two recordings about Chinese New Year. Chinese New Year, also known as the Spring Festival, is the longest and most important Chinese festival. It is celebrated in Chinese communities all over the world in January or February each year.

Track 7.1: Preparations for New Year

In this recording, you will hear Mu Lan describing her family's preparations for Chinese New Year. Listen to the recording carefully and then complete the exercise below.

Understanding

For each number in the paragraph below, choose the correct word from the list.

We are getting ready for Chinese New Year. Today, we **(1)** ____________ the whole house. Tomorrow, we'll make some red paper **(2)** ____________ – red for **(3)** ____________! Then my whole family is coming home for a special **(4)** ____________ – even my uncle who lives in Rome is coming! The next morning will be New Year and we'll put on **(5)** ____________ and set off **(6)** ____________. There will be dancing **(7)** ____________ in the street and lots of loud **(8)** ____________.

1.	decorated	cleaned	painted
2.	fireworks	lanterns	clothes
3.	traditional	good luck	happy
4.	reunion meal	parade	dance
5.	decorations	new clothes	lanterns
6.	balloons	lanterns	firecrackers
7.	meal	lions	decorations
8.	fireworks	balloons	meal

Track 7.2: New Year celebrations

You are going to listen to a radio interview about the Chinese New Year celebrations in Kowloon, Hong Kong. Listen to the recording carefully and then answer the questions below.

Understanding

For each question, choose the answer that fits best.

1. Where is the interviewer?
   a in a radio studio **b** in Shanghai **c** in Kowloon
2. Why did Yin Ning spend time in London?
   a she visited family there
   b she was a student there
   c she had a job there
3. Why do so many Chinese go home at New Year? Choose the answer that fits best.
   a because they think it is important to be with their family
   b because they think a spring clean is important
   c because they enjoy fireworks
4. Which three things does Yin Ning say bring good luck?
   a gold lettering, reunion meals and the colour red
   b the colour red, the noise of fireworks and cleaning the house
   c the noise of fireworks, reunion meals and the colour red

Challenge

Listen again to Track 7.2. Imagine you were in Kowloon central square during the New Year celebrations. Write an informal email to a friend describing the event. Include some of the new words you have learned about Chinese New Year and remember to use powerful adjectives to describe the exciting things you saw. Write about 100 words.

Speaking

Imagine you met Yin Ning in Kowloon during the Chinese New Year celebrations.

1. Think of three questions you would ask Yin Ning and share your questions with a partner.
2. With your partner, role play an interview with Yin Ning. Remember to listen carefully to the answers your partner gives. You may need to ask more questions to make sure you understand. Swap roles when you have finished.

Conditional sentences

A **conditional sentence** is one in which one event depends on another. We use conditional sentences to talk about things that might happen or could happen. Conditional sentences often include the word **'if'**.

Examples: **If** you put on your coat, you can come with me.
If you put your coat on, you will be warm.

Notice how we use a comma between the conditional clause (the clause beginning with 'if') and the main clause. In negative sentences, we can use 'if … not' or 'unless'.

Examples: **If** you do **not** put on your coat, you can't come with me.
Unless you put on your coat, you can't come with me.

When we want to talk about imaginary, unlikely or impossible situations in the present, we use:

If + past simple + would/could + infinitive

Examples: **If** I had lot of money, I **would** visit Japan.
If I knew your number, I **would** phone you.

Using conditional sentences

A Match the conditional clauses on the left with the clauses on the right. Then write out the sentences putting commas and full stops in the right place.

If you go to bed late	I would go for a walk
If they had a car	you could visit me more often
If I had more time	they would drive you there
Unless you finish your homework	you will be tired in the morning
If you lived near me	it would be more reliable
If it wasn't so cold	you can't watch television
If my computer wasn't so old	I would go to the party

B Fill the gaps in the following sentences with the correct form of the verbs in the word box.

have visit know lose

1. If I ____________ my phone, I would be very worried.
2. If we ____________ the answer, we would tell you.
3. If I ____________ some wings, I would fly to the moon.
4. If I ____________ China at New Year, I would enjoy the celebrations.

'If only' and 'wish'

To talk about present situations that we would like to be different, we often use **if only** or **wish** followed by the past simple.

Examples: I **wish** it wasn't raining.
If only I had less homework.

We also use 'wish' or 'if only' with 'could' or 'would' to talk about something in the present that we would like to change or to complain about something.

Examples: I **wish** they **wouldn't** play their music so loudly!
If only he **would** listen to me!
I **wish** I **could** find my phone.

Using 'if only' and 'wish'

A Fill the gaps in the following sentences with the correct forms of the verbs in brackets.

1. If only I ______________ in Hong Kong with you. (be)
2. He wishes he ______________ a better job. (have)
3. If only they ______________ English. (speak)
4. I wish I ______________ your number. (know)

B Fill the gaps in the following sentences.

1. I wish I ______________ speak Spanish.
2. If only it ______________ stop raining.
3. I wish she ______________ reply to my email.
4. I wish I ______________ help you.

C Complete the following sentences with your own words.

1. I wish you ____.
2. If only I ____.
3. He wishes he ____.
4. They wish they ____.

Traditional festivals

The start of the New Year is celebrated all around the world. Many countries also hold traditional festivals that to celebrate the arrival of spring. Some festivals are held at harvest time, when corn, fruit and other crops are gathered. Traditional festivals often include music, singing, dancing, special clothes and food. Look at the photographs below and then complete the tasks that follow.

Speaking

1. In small groups, look at the pictures on page 114 and match them to the captions below.

Hanami, or the Cherry Blossom Festival, is held in Japan between the end of March and early May. It celebrates the time when the cherry trees are in flower.

The Chapchar Kut is a harvest festival held in Northern India. People wear traditional headbands with feathers attached. A traditional dance is performed called the Cheraw or bamboo dance.

Holi is an ancient spring festival, celebrated in February or March each year by many communities in South Asia as well as outside Asia. The festivities include a carnival of colours, when people cover each other with dry powder and coloured water.

Chuseok is a traditional harvest festival held in Korea. Family members return to their hometowns, exchange gifts and share special food. Children dress in traditional silk clothes and there are musical performances with dancing and singing.

Nowruz is a traditional spring festival celebrated in Iran and many other countries. During the festivities, people visit each other and gather round a table, specially laid with delicious traditional food.

The Mid-Autumn Festival is a harvest festival celebrated in many countries, including China, Vietnam, Singapore and Malaysia. Families and friends come together and give thanks for the harvest. Lanterns play an important part in the festival.

2. The 'culture' of a community or country includes its beliefs and values, as well as its customs and traditions. Many traditional festivals and other customs date back for hundreds or even thousands of years. In small groups, discuss the following questions.

a Is it important to keep traditional festivals and customs going today? Why?

b Is it important to learn about the customs and traditions of other cultures? Why?

Challenge

Write two paragraphs describing a traditional festival that is held in your own country. What events and activities does it involve? Are special clothes worn? Does it include dancing and music and traditional food? Try to include some of the new words and phrases about customs and festivals that you have learned in this unit.

Reading corner: The Boab Festival

You are going to read a poem about the Boab Festival, which is held every year in Western Australia to celebrate nature and the history and culture of the Aboriginal people of Australia. The tree in the poem has a huge, thick trunk with a hollow, like a cave, inside. Read the poem and then answer the questions that follow.

Tree Festival

On the landscapes of Australia
the **weirdest** shapes appear,
so many **freaks** of nature
that only **flourish** here.

There's one found in the north-west,
no **odder** sight you'll see:
a **relic** of the Dreamtime
is the **mighty** Boab tree.

Out near the Fitroy River
a **grim** old tale they tell,
how one great **hollow** Boab
became a prison cell.

But now, when **wattle**'s **blooming**,
each year the people **throng**
to join the Boab Festival,
for sport and dance and song,

And some will hold their picnics
near a tribe's **Corroboree** –
it's like a kind of **tribute**
to the mighty Boab tree.

David Bateson

Glossary

blooming flowering

Corroboree an event celebrated with dance and music by Aboriginal people of Australia

flourish to grow strongly

freaks very strange things, animals or people

grim frightening or not nice

hollow having an empty space inside

mighty very strong

odder more unusual

relic something that has survived from an ancient time

throng come together in a crowd

tribute something said or done as a mark of respect or admiration

wattle a tree with a bright yellow flower

weirdest most strange

Understanding

Answer the following questions.

1. Where in Australia is this boab tree?
2. What is in flower during the Boab Festival?
3. Name four things that people do during the Boab Festival.
4. Write a sentence describing the poem's rhyming pattern.

Writing workshop: Writing a poem

You are going to write a poem about a custom, celebration or festival. It could be about a birthday or New Year celebration, a festival to celebrate a season, or another kind of festival that you have been to or one you have heard about.

Planning your poem

Before you start writing, decide what kind of custom or celebration you want to write about. Re-read the poem 'Tree Festival'. Find some words and phrases that the poet uses to describe the tree and the setting of the poem. Think about how the poet describes what people do during the festival. He doesn't tell a long story. Instead he hints at what happens, building up a picture in our minds with words and phrases.

Now think about your own poem. Think about the following:

- What is the custom, celebration or festival?
- Where does the custom or celebration happen? How will you describe the setting?
- At what time of year does it take place?
- What happens? Remember, you don't have to give all the details.
- What style of poem will you write? Will it rhyme?
- What words and phrases will you use to show the excitement that people feel?

Remember

You can use a thesaurus to help you find interesting verbs and adjectives for your poem. Try to choose words that will help to build up a picture in the reader's mind.

Writing, editing and proofreading

Now write your poem. Remember to use powerful words and phrases and try to create a picture in the readers' minds. Write a poem with three verses.

When you have finished your poem, read it to check for any mistakes in spelling or punctuation. Now read your poem out loud. Are you happy with they way it sounds? Can you change anything to make it better? Share your poem with a partner. Can they suggest any ways in which it can be improved?

Progress check

1. What unusual activity is sometimes part of birthday celebrations in Jamaica? Choose the correct answer.
   a ears are pulled **b** flour is thrown (1 mark)

2. What are hundreds and thousands?
   a decorations made from sugar
   b fairy bread (1 mark)

3. Use the following prepositions before nouns, pronouns or noun phrases to make four prepositional phrases.
   a under **b** across **c** without **d** between (4 marks)

4. Write four sentences using the prepositional phrases you made in question 4. (4 marks)

5. Which of the following statements is correct?
   a She did her best work like a teacher.
   b She did her best work as a teacher. (1 mark)

6. Which colour is used for luck in Chinese New Year decorations?
   a blue **b** yellow **c** red (1 mark)

7. Write three sentences about Chinese New Year. (3 marks)

8. Use 'if only' or 'wish' to complete the following sentences
   a ______________ I had more time.
   b ______________ you hadn't been late, you would have seen the performance.
   c ______________ he had read the instructions, he would know what to do. (3 marks)

9. What is it said a boab tree was once used as? (1 mark)

10. Write three sentences describing a festival or celebration of your own choice. (6 marks)

(Total: 25 marks)

Progress assessment

		🙂	😐	🙁
Reading skills	I can understand specific information in a text.	O	O	O
	I can understand the meaning in a text, even if it is not stated directly.	O	O	O
Use of English skills	I can use a range of prepositions in prepositional phrases.	O	O	O
	I can use if, unless, if only and wish clauses.	O	O	O
Listening skills	I can understand specific information in what someone is saying.	O	O	O
	I can understand the meaning of what someone is saying, even if it is not stated directly.	O	O	O
Speaking skills	I can give an opinion on a range of topics.	O	O	O
	I can ask questions to help me understand clearly what someone means.	O	O	O
Writing skills	I can plan and draft written work with some support.	O	O	O
	I can write, edit and proofread written work with some support.	O	O	O

✓ Action plan

Reading: I need to ______________________________

Use of English: I need to ______________________________

Listening: I need to ______________________________

Speaking: I need to ______________________________

Writing: I need to ______________________________

I would like to know more about ______________________________

8 Cookbook

In this chapter you will:

Explore
- traditional dishes
- recipes for different occasions

Create
- a recipe
- a book review

Engage
- with meaning not actually stated
- with attitudes and opinions

Collaborate
- on ideas for a cookbook
- to give a presentation

Reflect
- on relative clauses
- on present forms with future meaning

I am just someone who likes cooking, and for whom sharing food is a form of expression. Maya Angelou, American author

If you want to make a friend, go to someone's house and eat with him ... the people who give you their food give you their heart. Cesar Chavez, founder of the American Farm Workers' Association

For me, cooking is an expression of the land where you are and the culture of that place. Wolfgang Puck, chef

Thinking ahead

1. Have you ever used a cookbook? Why do people use cookbooks?
2. Which is your favourite meal? What do you like most about it?
3. Do you prefer sweet dishes or savoury dishes?

Word builder

Complete the following tasks.

1. Match the words on the left to the correct meaning on the right.

bake	a device used to weigh something
ingredients	how hot or cold something is
scales	to cook in an oven
weigh	to measure how heavy something is
temperature	things you mix together to cook something

2. Use the words from question 1 to fill the gaps in the following paragraph.

   When you ______________ cakes or biscuits, it is important to ______________ the ______________ carefully. You will need ______________ for this. For good results, you should make sure your oven is at the right ______________.

Speaking

Discuss the following questions with a partner. Listen to your partner's opinions and ask questions to make sure you understand.

1. Do you like to help with the cooking before a meal?
2. What three things would you like to learn to cook?
3. Do you think people should always use a recipe when they are cooking?

Cookie recipe

Read the following recipe for chocolate chip cookies and then answer the questions that follow.

Chocolate chip cookies

Ingredients

125g unsalted butter, softened
150g light brown sugar
1 egg
175g plain flour
½ teaspoon baking powder
pinch of salt
175g chocolate chips

Makes about 18 cookies.

Method

1. First, line two baking sheets with baking paper and **heat** the oven to 190°C/375°F.
2. Then, put the softened butter and sugar into a large mixing bowl. **Beat** with a wooden spoon or electric mixer until the mixture is light and **fluffy**.
3. Next, beat in the egg, a little at a time.
4. After that, add the flour, baking powder and salt and stir gently until everything is mixed well.
5. Then, add the chocolate chips and mix well.
6. Now, using a teaspoon, place spoonfuls of the mixture onto the lined baking sheets.
7. During baking, the mixture will **spread** so leave plenty of room around each spoonful of cookie **dough**.
8. Bake in the oven for 12–15 minutes until pale golden.
9. Use oven gloves to remove the baking sheets from the oven and let the cookies cool slightly before moving them to a wire rack to cool completely.
10. Store in an **airtight** container for up to four days.

Glossary

airtight not letting air in or out

beat to stir quickly

dough a thick mixture of flour and other ingredients

fluffy soft and light

heat to make something hot

spread move to cover a bigger area

Understanding

A Answer the following questions.

1. How many cookies will this recipe make?
2. What is the first thing you should do after beating together the sugar and butter? Choose the correct answer.
   - **a** add the egg
   - **b** stir in the flour and chocolate chips
   - **c** add the baking powder and egg
3. Which two ingredients need to be added to the mixture at the same time as the flour?
   - **a** the salt and eggs
   - **b** the baking powder and chocolate chips
   - **c** the salt and baking powder

B Answer the following questions.

1. What do you think would happen if you did not leave enough space around the spoonfuls of cookie mixture?
2. Why do you think each step of the recipe has a number by it?
3. Find four examples of verbs that tell you what to do (imperative or command verbs) in the recipe.

Writing

You are going to write a recipe of your own. First think of a dish you like to eat. What ingredients does it include? How do you think you would cook the dish? Write your own recipe, making the instructions as clear as you can.

When you have written your recipe, read it carefully and correct any mistakes. Then show it to a partner. Can they suggest any improvements?

Challenge

Imagine you have decided you want to cook some chocolate chip cookies. You have all the ingredients listed in the recipe on page 122 except for eggs and baking powder. Use the Internet or cookbooks you have at home or in a library to find out the answer to the question 'Can you make chocolate chip cookies without eggs or baking powder?' Then write two sentences explaining what you have found out.

Remember

Remember to include the following features in your recipe:

- a title that states what the recipe is for
- a list of ingredients – what you need
- the method – what you need to do
- clearly numbered steps, with each step set out on a new line
- words such as 'first', 'next', 'then' and 'finally' to make the instructions easy to follow
- imperative or command verbs (for example 'put', 'add', 'pour').

Reported speech

When we want to tell someone what another person said, we often use **reported speech**. Compare the following sentences:

"I am baking some cookies," said Mara. (direct speech)

Mara **said she was** baking some cookies. (reported speech)

Mara **told me that she was** baking some cookies. (reported speech)

In reported speech, we do not use speech marks and we sometimes use the word 'that' before the reported words.

We often change the tense of the verb in reported speech. In the examples above, "I am baking" changes to the past continuous, 'she was baking'. The present simple often changes to the past simple.

Example: "The oven **is** too hot," said Mara. → Mara said the oven **was** too hot.

The past simple often stays the same, but sometimes we change it to the past perfect.

Examples: "I **baked** some cookies," said Mara.
Mara said she **baked** some cookies.
Mara told me that she **had baked** some cookies.

Using reported speech

A Change the sentences below to reported speech, using 'said' or 'told'. The first one has been done for you.

1. "I am adding some more chocolate chips" said Paulo. Paulo said that he was adding some more chocolate chips.
2. "I need some more flour," Mara said.
3. "It is important to add the eggs gradually," the chef told us.
4. "The cookies are ready," said Paulo.

B Change the following sentences into reported speech, using the past simple. The first one has been done for you.

1. "I heated up the oven first,' said Paulo. Paulo said he heated up the oven first.
2. "I ate all the cookies," said Mara.
3. "I baked the cookies until they were golden brown," she told me.
4. "I added too many chocolate chips," said Paulo.

C Change the sentences in B to reported speech using the past perfect.

Remember

We make the past perfect by using 'had' before the past participle.

Examples: had cooked/had made/had put/had wanted.

Reported commands, requests and questions

When someone tells us to do something in direct speech, they give us an order or **command**. In reported commands, we use 'told' with the 'to' infinitive form of the verb.

Example: "**Heat** the oven up first," he said. → He **told me to heat** the oven up first.

When someone asks us to do something, they make a **request**. In reported speech, we use 'asked' + somebody + the 'to' infinitive.

Example: "Will you buy some more flour?" she asked me. → She **asked me to buy** some more flour.

In reported **questions**, we can use 'if' or 'whether'. When there is a question word, such as 'what' or 'how' in the question, we use the question word in the reported question.

Examples: "Do you like these cookies?" she asked. → She **asked whether** I liked the cookies.
"How many are there?" she asked. → She asked **how many** there were.

Using reported commands, requests and questions

Remember

Requests for objects can be turned into reported speech using 'asked for'.

Example: "Can I have a cookie?" he asked. → He asked for a cookie.

A Fill the gaps with the correct forms of the verbs in brackets.

1. She told me ____________ the cookies out of the oven. (take)
2. She asked me ____________ with her. (go)
3. He asked me whether I ____________ another cookie. (want)

B For each question, choose the correct reported speech sentence.

1. "Did you close the oven door?"
   - a She told me to close the oven door.
   - b She asked me whether I had closed the oven door.
   - c She said that I should close the oven door.
2. "Can I have another one?"
   - a She asked for another one.
   - b She said she wanted another one.
   - c She wanted another one.
3. "Why are there are no cookies left?"
   - a She asked why there were no cookies left.
   - b She said there were no cookies left.
   - c She told me why there were no cookies left.

Class cookbook

Implied meaning, opinions and attitudes

Sometimes in our writing or when we speak, we suggest something but we don't say it openly. The meaning of what we are saying is **implied**. When someone is speaking, the tone of their voice or the words they choose can give us clues about what they mean, as well as about their attitudes and opinions. For example, if we don't agree with someone, we may not say so. The tone of our voice may change and we may use phrases such as 'That's not a bad idea, but …' or 'Possibly, but …'.

Track 8.1: Favourite recipes

You are going to listen to a recording in which Chloe and Alexa talk about recipes for a class cookbook. Listen to their opinions and answer the questions that follow.

Understanding

A For each question, choose the correct answer.

1. What kind of ideas for recipes has Chloe?
   - **a** brownies, cookies and cupcakes
   - **b** biscuits, cakes or sweets
2. What kinds of recipes does Alexa want to include?
   - **a** tasty and quick
   - **b** easy to make and fun

B For each question, choose the correct answer.

1. What word or phrase does Alexa use to show she agrees they should include recipes to make when friends visit?
   - **a** That's an idea
   - **b** Exactly
2. How do we know that Alexa does not agree that the cookbook should just include recipes for party food?
   - **a** She says "That's an idea, but why party food?"
   - **b** She says "That's not a bad idea, Chloe, but I don't know."

Track 8.2: Class cookbook

The teacher has asked the students to suggest a good title for the class cookbook. Listen carefully to Chloe and Alexa's ideas and answer the questions that follow.

Understanding

A For each question, choose the correct answer.

1. What is the first title that Chloe suggests?
   - **a** Clever Cooking
   - **b** Clever Class Cookbook
2. Which recipe does Alexa suggest for the cookbook?
   - **a** apple and banana muffins
   - **b** apple and banana smoothie

B For each question, choose the correct answer.

1. What does Alexa think about the first title Chloe suggests?
   - **a** It isn't very easy to remember.
   - **b** It doesn't show the cookbook is for children.
2. Which of these statements would Chloe and Alexa say?
   - **a** We want the cookbook to include many different kinds of recipes.
   - **b** We only want to include healthy recipes in the cookbook.

Challenge

Rewrite the following parts of Chloe and Alexa's conversation as reported speech. The first part has been done for you.

1. Alexa: What are you thinking, Chloe? Alexa asked Chloe what she was thinking.
2. Chloe: 'Clever Cooking for Kids' is a great title.
3. Alexa: I've got a recipe for a mango and banana smoothie.
4. Chloe: You're right, Alexa.

Speaking

In small groups, plan an idea for a cookbook. Think about these questions:

- What will make your cookbook different from other cookbooks?
- What kind of recipes will it include?
- Why would people choose to buy it?

Now prepare a three-minute presentation, in which your group will explain your ideas to the class. The class will then decide whether the cookbook should be produced. Try to use words and phrases you have learned about cookbooks. Use language that will persuade them and explain what will be special about your cookbook.

Relative clauses

We use relative clauses to give more information about nouns or pronouns. Relative clauses make it clear which person or thing we mean. When we are talking about people, we use 'who' or 'that' after the noun.

Examples: I will ask my friend **who gave me the recipe**.
She is the person **that wrote the book**.

In the examples above, 'who gave me the recipe' and 'that wrote the book' are relative clauses. They give more information about 'my friend' and 'the person'.

When we are talking about things, we use 'that' or 'which'.

Examples: Where is the flour **that I bought**?
Here are the cookies **which we have baked**.

When we are giving a reason, we use **why**.

Example: The reason **why I am going out** is to buy some butter.

Using relative clauses

A Find the relative clauses in the sentences below.

1. Check you have all the ingredients that you need.
2. I bought a cookbook, which includes ideas for healthy salads.
3. She gave the sugar to her friend who was helping with the cooking.

B Add 'who', 'which', 'that' or 'why' to the sentences below.

1. This is a dish __________ is very easy to make.
2. I like to eat food __________ is healthy.
3. What is the name of the chef __________ wrote the book?
4. There are many reasons __________ people use cookbooks.

C Add the words 'who', 'that' or 'which' to fill the gaps in Chloe's message to Alexa.

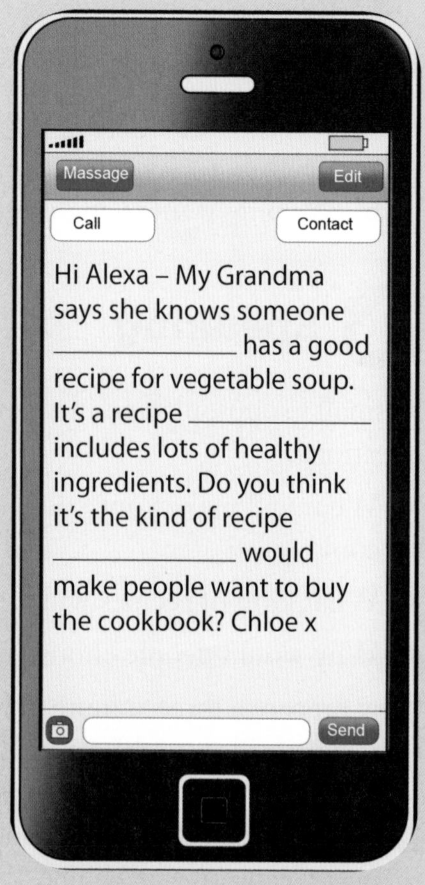

Present forms for the future

To talk about fixed arrangements and things that are planned for a particular time in the future, we often use the **present simple**.

Examples: My bus **leaves** in five minutes.
The film **starts** at at 5 o'clock.
The school term **ends** on Tuesday.

To talk about our plans and things we have arranged to do in the future, we can also use the **present continuous**. Remember, the present continuous is formed with a present form of the verb 'be' (am/is/are) and a present participle (ending in –ing).

Examples: I **am making** a meal for the family at the weekend.
My friend **is coming** tomorrow.
I **am going** to the theatre on Saturday.

Remember

See page 154–5 for more information on present simple and present continuous forms.

Using present forms for the future

A Choose the correct forms of the verbs in brackets to fill the gaps in these sentences.

1. The shop ____________ at 5.30 p.m. (close)
2. The programme ____________ in five minutes. (end)
3. I ____________ him on Saturday. (see)
4. The children ____________ with the cooking tonight. (help)

B Helen has asked Anna about her plans for the weekend. Rewrite Anna's message changing the verbs from the present simple to the present continuous.

C Look at the page from Helen's diary below. Write a message from Helen to Anna using present forms to tell her about her plans for the weekend.

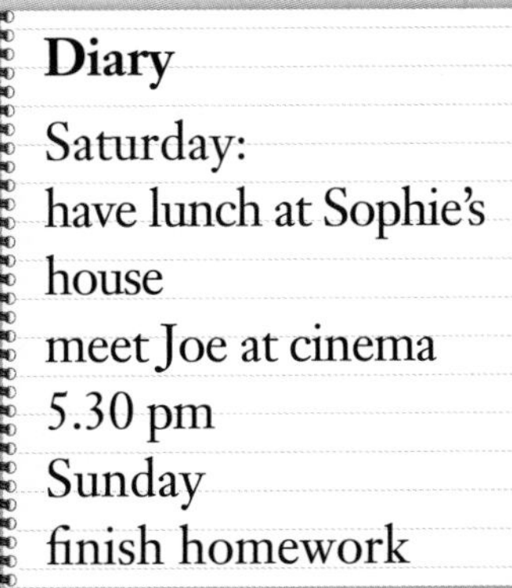

Favourite dishes around the world

The cuisine, or style of cooking, of a country or community is part of its culture, and many traditional dishes date back for hundreds of years. Look at the pictures below and then complete the tasks that follow.

2

Word builder

With a partner, discuss the meaning of the words on the left and match them with the definitions on the right.

culture	a style of cooking, especially in a particular community or country
cuisine	following or belonging to customs that have continued for a long time without changing
national	the ideas and customs of a particular country or community
traditional	to do with a particular country

National dishes

Working in small groups, complete the following tasks.

1. Discuss what each picture on page 130 shows and match the pictures to the captions below.

a Pizza comes from Italy. It consists of a round base of dough, topped with tomatoes, cheese and other ingredients.

b Kibbeh is one of the national dishes of Lebanon. It is a kind of meatball, made from meat, onion, spices and rice or cracked wheat.

c Empanadas are pastries filled with savoury ingredients. They come from Spain, and are popular in Argentina and other Latin American countries.

d Sushi is a dish that comes from Japan. It consists of small balls or rolls of cooked rice and other ingredients such as fish.

2. Discuss the following questions with your group.
   - **a** Does your country have any national or favourite dishes?
   - **b** How would you describe the traditional style of cooking in your community or country?

Performing poems

Complete the following tasks.

1. The poet Michael Rosen has written a poem about his favourite food, chocolate cake. You can watch him perform his poem on the Internet:

   www.michaelrosen.co.uk/myfamily_cake.html

   As you watch, notice the way Michael Rosen uses his voice, face, arms and hands to make the performance more interesting.
2. With a partner, choose a poem to perform to your class. Decide which lines you will say and which lines your partner will say. Practise reading the poem, using as much expression as you can. Then give your performance to the class.

Reading corner: Cookbook review

We can find out people's opinions about books by reading reviews. *Roald Dahl's Revolting Recipes* is a cookbook containing recipes inspired by the food that features in Roald Dahl's books for children. Read the online review of the cookbook and then answer the questions.

Roald Dahl's Revolting Recipes

Reviewer's rating *****

Revolting Recipes has recipes for 'Lickable Wallpaper', 'Stink Bugs Eggs' and 'Eatable Pillows'. All these foods can be found in *Charlie and the Chocolate Factory*, *James and the Giant Peach* and Roald Dahl's other books. The recipes are easy to make and lots of fun. There are also beautiful colour photographs to show all the delicious food.

I bought the book for my 11-year-old daughter. She loves it and we have made most of the recipes together. It has lots of different recipes in it so you should have a recipe for every occasion.

It was really great to see my daughter smile, as she is a fan of all Dahl's books, and naming each recipe after food that appears in the books makes it very special.

The book is excellent in every way and would also make a good gift, as it is very different from other cookbooks you can buy. It is also a reasonable price. I would recommend buying it.

Understanding

Answer the following questions.

1. What is 'Lickable Wallpaper'?
2. What is the writer's opinion of the cookbook? Choose the correct answer.
   - **a** She thinks it is a brilliant cookbook.
   - **b** She thinks it is the same as other cookbooks she has.
   - **c** She thinks it is quite good.
3. Why do you think the writer says 'I would recommend it'? Find as many reasons as you can in the review.

Writing workshop: Writing a review

You are going to write a review of a cookbook. It can be about a cookbook you have used, one you have at home or one you have seen on the Internet or in a library. Or you can make up a cookbook in your mind and write a review of that.

Remember

The purpose of a book review is to give some information about the book as well as your opinion about it. When you write a review, think about who will read it and what they will want to know about the book. Remember to give reasons for your opinions and try to use some of the vocabulary you have learned about cookbooks in this unit.

Planning your review

When you are planning your review, you need to think about the purpose of the review and the features you will include. First decide what you think about the book. What do you like about it? Is there anything you do not like? Make some notes about the information you will include. Think about these questions:

- What kind of recipes does it include?
- Is it easy to use? Are the recipes clear and easy to follow?
- Does it have colourful photographs?
- Which recipes would you like to try or have you tried?

Challenge

After you have written your cookbook review, look for words and phrases that are positive or negative. Think about antonyms for these words and then rewrite your review so that it gives the opposite opinion.

Writing, editing and proofeading

When you write your review, you may want to use the following structure:

Paragraph 1 Tell readers the title of the book and some general information, such as who wrote it and what kind of recipes it includes.

Paragraph 2 Give a bit more detail about the contents of the book, such as details about the layout, photographs or particular recipes you have tried or want to try.

Paragraph 3 Give your opinion about whether the book is good or not. Remember to explain the reasons for your opinion.

Paragraph 4 Write a short conclusion, summarising your opinion and saying whether you would recommend the book.

Write 100–150 words.

When you have finished your review, check your spelling, grammar and punctuation carefully and correct any mistakes. Ask a partner to read the review. Do they think you have made your opinions clear? Is there is anything you have left out that they would like to know?

Progress check ✓

1. Name three ingredients used in the chocolate chip cookie recipe, apart from chocolate chips. (3 marks)

2. Which two instructions are in the cookie recipe?
   - **a** Beat in the egg, a little at a time.
   - **b** Melt the butter in a saucepan.
   - **c** Bake in the oven for 12–15 minutes. (2 marks)

3. What kinds of recipes do Chloe and Alexa want to include in the class cookbook? (1 mark)

4. What is implied meaning? Choose the correct answer.
   - **a** meaning that is suggested but not directly stated
   - **b** the tone of someone's voice (1 mark)

5. Change the following sentences into reported speech.
   - **a** "I cooked the meal," he told me.
   - **b** "Please close the door," she asked. (2 marks)

6. Add 'which', 'who' or 'that' to the following sentences.
   - **a** I like recipes ____________ are easy to follow.
   - **b** Have you heard of the chef ____________ wrote the book? (2 marks)

7. Change the verbs in these sentences to the present continuous.
   - **a** They meet you tomorrow at the airport.
   - **b** We play football on Sunday. (2 marks)

8. For each sentence, write down whether you think the writer would recommend the cookbook.
   - **a** I think there are too many ingredients for each recipe.
   - **b** When will I ever make that kind of food? (2 marks)

9. Write down four things you should include in a book review. (4 marks)

10. Write three sentences giving an opinion about a book you have read. (6 marks)

(Total: 25 marks)

Progress assessment

		🙂	😐	🙁
Reading skills	I can recognise the attitude or opinion of a writer.	O	O	O
	I can recognise features of instructions.	O	O	O
Use of English skills	I can use the present simple and present continuous with future meaning.	O	O	O
	I can use relative clauses.	O	O	O
	I can use reported speech forms.	O	O	O
Listening skills	I can understand the detail of what someone is saying.	O	O	O
	I can understand what is implied but not actually said.	O	O	O
Speaking skills	I can work with my peers on classroom tasks.	O	O	O
	I can use words and phrases that relate to the topic I am studying.	O	O	O
Writing skills	I can use the appropriate style for a book review.	O	O	O
	I can use accurate grammar in my writing.	O	O	O

✓ Action plan

Reading: I need to ______

Use of English: I need to ______

Listening: I need to ______

Speaking: I need to ______

Writing: I need to ______

I would like to know more about ______

9 Communication

Explore
- different ways of communicating
- the history of the telephone

Create
- an email
- a diary entry

Engage
- with a famous inventor
- with non-verbal communication

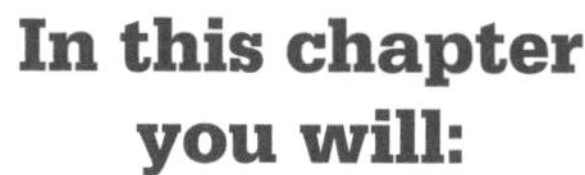

In this chapter you will:

Collaborate
- to research different kinds of signals
- to prepare a presentation

Reflect
- on the use of infinitive forms
- on phrasal and prepositonal verbs

The most important thing in communication is hearing what isn't said. Peter Drucker, author

We have two ears and one mouth so that we can listen twice as much as we speak. Epictetus, Ancient Greek philosopher

When people talk, listen completely. Most people never listen. Ernest Hemingway, writer

Thinking ahead

1. What different ways do you use to communicate with people? How many ways can you think of?
2. Why is it important to communicate?
3. Do we always need to use words to communicate?

Word builder

Use words from the box to fill the gaps in the following paragraph.

signals	technology	satellites	information
Internet	text	smile	

Communication is the passing on of ____________ and ideas. We communicate with each other in many different ways, from a ____________ on our face to ____________ and messages sent over the ____________. We often use ____________ to communicate, for example by telephone, television, email, ____________ message or ____________ that send back information from space.

Speaking

With a partner, discuss the following questions.

1. How often do you use technology to communicate? How often do you send text messages to your friends and how often do you send emails?
2. Why do you choose to use technology to communicate with people?
3. Imagine you could not use any kind of technology to communicate for a whole day. How would you feel? How would you communicate with people on that day?
4. What do you think is the best way of communicating with someone?

The first telephone call

Read the following information about the first telephone call and then answer the questions that follow.

"Mr Watson, come here – I want to see you." These were the first words ever spoken on the telephone. They were spoken by the famous scientist and inventor Alexander Graham Bell. He made the call from his laboratory in Boston, USA, to his assistant, who was in the next room.

Bell's wife lost her ability to hear when she was a child, and Bell was very interested in hearing and how sounds are communicated. He wondered if the sound of the human voice could be sent, or transmitted, down a wire. He decided to try. Bell's diary entry tells us what happened.

March 10 1876

… I then shouted into the **mouthpiece** the following sentence: "Mr Watson, come here – I want to see you." To my delight he came and **declared** that he had heard and understood what I said.

I asked him to repeat the words. He answered, "You said, "Mr Watson, come here – I want to see you." We then changed places and I listened at the **speaker** while Mr Watson read a few passages from a book into the mouthpiece … The effect was loud but **indistinct** and **muffled**.

The words were indistinct and muffled but history had been made. Bell was one of a number of scientists and inventors who contributed to the development of the telephone. By 1886, over 150,000 people owned telephones and that number just kept on growing.

Glossary

declared said something clearly

indistinct not clear

mouthpiece the part of the telephone you speak into

muffled made quieter and less clear

speaker the part of some equipment that sound comes from

transmitted when technology is used to send and receive sound (for example in radio or television)

Understanding

A For each question, choose the correct answer.

1. Who heard the first words spoken on the telephone?
   - **a** Mr Watson **b** Alexander Graham Bell
2. When did this happen?
   - **a** 1876 **b** 1886 **c** we are not told
3. What had Bell been trying to do?
   - **a** transmit sound through a wire
   - **b** understand the different sounds of the human voice

B For each question, choose the answer that fits best.

1. What was the first thing that happened that made Bell think the experiment had worked?
   - **a** Mr Watson came into his room and said he had heard and understood what Bell had said.
   - **b** Bell heard the sound of his own voice.
2. What phrase best describes the sound of those first calls?
   - **a** quiet but clear
   - **b** loud but unclear
   - **c** clear and loud

C How do you think Bell felt when Watson came into his room? How do you know?

Challenge

A lot has happened to the telephone since the day of the first telephone call in 1876. Find out on the Internet or in a library about the history of the telephone. Then prepare a wallchart or poster with a timeline of important dates and developments for the telephone.

Writing

How important is the telephone in your life? Alexander Graham Bell died in 1922, but imagine you could meet him. What would you ask him? What would you tell him about telephones today? Write a blog entry describing what happened. Remember to describe how you felt and what you thought about the day. Write about 100 words.

Verbs and adjectives followed by infinitives

Many verbs are followed by the 'to' infinitive form of a verb.

Examples: He **wants to go** out.
She **decided to send** an email.

Other verbs that are followed by the 'to' infinitive include:

agree, choose, expect, forget, hope, learn, need, offer, plan, promise, refuse, remember

We also use the 'to' infinitive after many adjectives.

Examples: I was **glad to get** your email.
It is **difficult to hear** you.

Other adjectives that can be followed by the 'to' infinitive include:

dangerous, easy, excited, good, happy, hard, pleased, possible, sad, sorry, surprised

Using 'to' infinitives after verbs and adjectives

A Use an adjective or the correct form of a verb from the word box to complete the following sentences.

pleased take understand

1. He said he was __________ to win the race.
2. She was speaking very quickly, so I found it hard __________ what she was saying.
3. Did you remember __________ your book home?

B Complete the following sentences using the correct form of the two verbs in brackets.

1. She looked at the menu and __________ a pizza. (decide/order)
2. Please __________ more careful next time. (remember/be)
3. After the lesson he __________ his book home. (forget/take)

C Choose two verbs and two adjectives from the word box. Then use the words with the 'to' infinitive in two sentences of your own.

Verbs	Adjectives
choose	dangerous
want	excited
hope	surprised
learn	easy

–ing forms after verbs and prepositions

Some verbs are followed by the –ing form of a verb instead of an infinitive.

Example: I **enjoy swimming** (not 'I enjoy to swim.')

In Unit 5 you learned that –ing forms are often used as nouns. In the sentence above, notice how the –ing form ('swimming') is acting as a noun. It is the object of the verb 'enjoy' ('swimming' is the name of the thing I enjoy).

Other verbs that are followed by the –ing form of a verb include:

dislike, finish, like, love, mind, stop, suggest

We often use –ing forms after prepositions (at/in/for/on/with, etc). We cannot use an infinitive form after a preposition.

Example: I am not very good **at swimming**. (not 'I am not very good at to swim.')

In the above example, 'swimming' is acting as a noun and the object that follows the preposition.

Using –ing forms after verbs and prepositions

A Use the correct forms of the verbs in brackets to fill the gaps in the sentences. The first one has been done for you.

1. He ______________ the book yesterday. (finish/read) He finished reading the book yesterday.
2. Would you ______________ more slowly? (mind/speak)
3. I ______________ to music. (like/listen)

B Complete the sentences below using a word from the word box and the correct form of the verb in brackets.

for   to   after

1. I played basketball ______________ my homework. (finish)
2. He is looking forward ______________ you. (meet)
3. I thanked my friend ______________ me. (help)

C Finish the following sentences with your own words using the –ing form of a verb.

1. I prefer ________________________________
2. I am sorry for ________________________________
3. I am thinking of ________________________________

Remember

Prepositions are always followed by an object. This can be a noun, a noun phrase, a pronoun or the –ing form of a verb.

Examples:

I put the flowers **on the table**.

I went to the cinema **with them**.

Signalling

You are going to listen to some recordings about different kinds of signals that are used to communicate information. Before you listen to the recordings, complete the Word builder activity below.

Word builder

Use the words in the word box to fill the gaps in the paragraph below.

movements signal guide travellers instructions

A ______________ is a way of communicating information or ______________ from one person or place to another. Signals can be ______________, actions or sounds. Many kinds of signals are used to ______________, warn or simply inform ______________.

Track 9.1: Smoke signals

Listen to the recording and answer the questions.

1. What were smoke signals used for?
2. What could be seen from far away when people lit bonfires on high points?

Track 9.2: Flags at sea

Listen to the recording and answer the questions.

1. What is the name of the signalling system used at sea? Choose the correct answer.
   - **a** the Blue Peter system
   - **b** the International Code of Signals
2. Which one of these is the Blue Peter flag?

a

b

c

Track 9.3: Flag semaphore

Listen to the recording and answer the questions.

1. Why does a semaphore signaller hold flags in different positions? Choose the answer that fits best.
   - **a** to spell out messages
   - **b** so other ships can see the flags moving
   - **c** to signal that a ship is ready to sail
2. What is used at night instead of flags?

Track 9.4: Traffic signals

Listen to the recording and answer the questions.

1. Where were the first electric traffic lights set up? Choose the correct answer.
   - **a** London
   - **b** the USA
   - **c** no one knows
2. What does an amber or yellow light indicate on a traffic signal?
   - **a** it is safe to cross the road
   - **b** go
   - **c** a warning
3. Which features are included in the recording?
   - **a** opinions, facts and informal language
   - **b** facts, formal language and clear sentences
   - **c** facts, informal language and clear sentences

Glossary

adapted changed for a different purpose
explosion when something suddenly blows apart
flow steady movement
gas lamps a lamp that burns gas to make light
junctions points where two or more things, such as roads, meet
pedestrian crossings points on a road where people can cross safely
wands thin sticks or rods

Challenge

Choose one form of signalling described in the recordings and find out more about it on the Internet or in a library. See what you can discover about:

- its history
- where it was developed
- how it worked
- what it looked like.

Plan a presentation to the class to explain what you have found out. Give your presentation to the class and then answer any questions your classmates may have.

Phrasal verbs

A **phrasal verb** is made up of two parts: a main verb and a word such as 'in', 'out', 'up', 'down', 'off', 'away'. When they are used as part of a phrasal verb, these words are called 'particles'.

Examples: The boy **ran away**.
I watched the plane **take off**.

Sometimes, a phrasal verb has an object. Sometimes, the object comes after the phrasal verb. Sometimes it comes between the two parts of the verb.

Examples: I put on **my coat**.
I put **my coat** on.

If the object is a pronoun, the pronoun must come between the two parts of the verb.

Example: I put **it** on. (not 'I put on it').

Sometimes a phrasal verb is followed by a preposition.

Examples: He looked up **at** the sky.
I walked in **through** the door.

Using phrasal verbs

A Complete the following sentences using a word from the word box.

off on down

1. The traffic lights turned green, so he drove ___________.
2. I was late because my bus broke ___________.
3. Signals are used to pass ___________ messages.

B Complete the following message from Paula to Sara. Use the words from the box below.

up away off

From: Paula

To: Sara

I had to leave work early today. Please could you turn my computer ___________? Also, please can you put my diary ___________? Thanks for putting ___________ with me! See you tomorrow.

Paula

Prepositional verbs

Prepositional verbs are formed with a verb and a preposition (such as 'to', 'about', 'with', 'in', 'on', etc).

Example: verb **listen** + preposition **to** = listen to

Unlike phrasal verbs, prepositional verbs always have an object. The object always comes straight after the preposition. A prepositional verb cannot be separated. This means we cannot put the object between the verb and the preposition.

The object of a prepositional verb can be a noun, a noun phrase, a pronoun or the –ing form of a verb.

Examples: He always listens to you.
I often think about travelling.

In the above examples 'you' and 'travelling' are the objects of the prepositional verbs 'listens to' and 'think about'.

Using prepositional verbs

A Use the prepositions in the word box to complete the sentences below.

to with about on

1. I am talking ____________ my friend on the phone.
2. She told me she was thinking ____________ having a holiday.
3. The train driver depends ____________ the signals.
4. I agree ____________ everything you have said.

B Complete Filipe's message below using the correct form of a prepositional verb from the box.

get off decide on wait for agree with

From: Filipe
To: Sandro
Just to let you know, we will ____________ you at the airport. Have you ____________ your plans for dinner? I ____________ Jamal that we should all go out for a special dinner. See you when you ____________ the plane!
Filipe

Challenge

Write three sentences of your own using the prepositional verbs from the word box.

look for
rely on
deal with

Communicating without words

We often show attitudes and opinions without using words. Look at the following picture and then complete the tasks that follow.

Word builder

Use words from the box to fill the gaps in the paragraph.

face-to-face	non-verbal	body language
hands	gestures	expressions

When we communicate with people ______________, we can use words. We can also use our face, ______________ and arms to show how we are feeling. This is called '______________'. Examples of body language include ______________, ______________ and eye movements. Body language is an important form of ______________ communication.

Speaking

A In a small group, discuss the following questions.

1. How can we use body language to show the following emotions?
   - **a** happiness
   - **b** surprise
   - **c** anger
2. What other emotions can we show using expressions on our face or other kinds of body language?

B In a small group, look at the picture of the school council meeting on page 146 and discuss the following questions.

1. How many students at the meeting are listening to what the speaker is saying? How do you know?
2. Do you think any of the students disagree with what the speaker is saying? How do you know?
3. Are any of the students thinking about other things at the meeting? How do you know?

C In a small group, discuss the following questions.

1. In some countries, people nod their heads to show agreement and shake their heads if they disagree. What gestures do people use in your country to show they agree or disagree?
2. Why might you choose to use a gesture such as nodding your head during a discussion rather than words?
3. Why is it important to listen to other people's opinions during a discussion?
4. How can you use body language to show you are listening to someone and that you are interested in what they are saying?

Remember

During your discussions, remember to ask questions to show you are interested in what the other members of your group are saying. You can ask the person who is speaking questions such as 'Why do you think that ...?' or 'Can you explain why ... '. You can also ask the whole group questions such as 'Does everyone agree?'.

Reading corner: Guitar lessons

Marcos wants to learn to play the guitar. One day he sees an advertisement on the school noticeboard. He wants to find out more. Read the advertisement and the emails below and then answer the questions.

Free lessons! Learn to play the guitar!

Expert tuition from a specialist player and teacher.
No experience needed.
For more information email: jayguitar@stringtuit.org

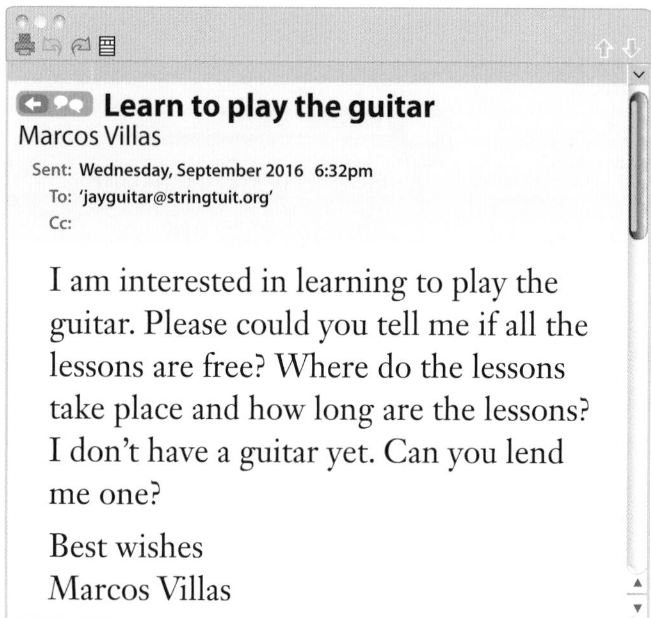

Learn to play the guitar
Marcos Villas
Sent: Wednesday, September 2016 6:32pm
To: 'jayguitar@stringtuit.org'
Cc:

I am interested in learning to play the guitar. Please could you tell me if all the lessons are free? Where do the lessons take place and how long are the lessons? I don't have a guitar yet. Can you lend me one?

Best wishes
Marcos Villas

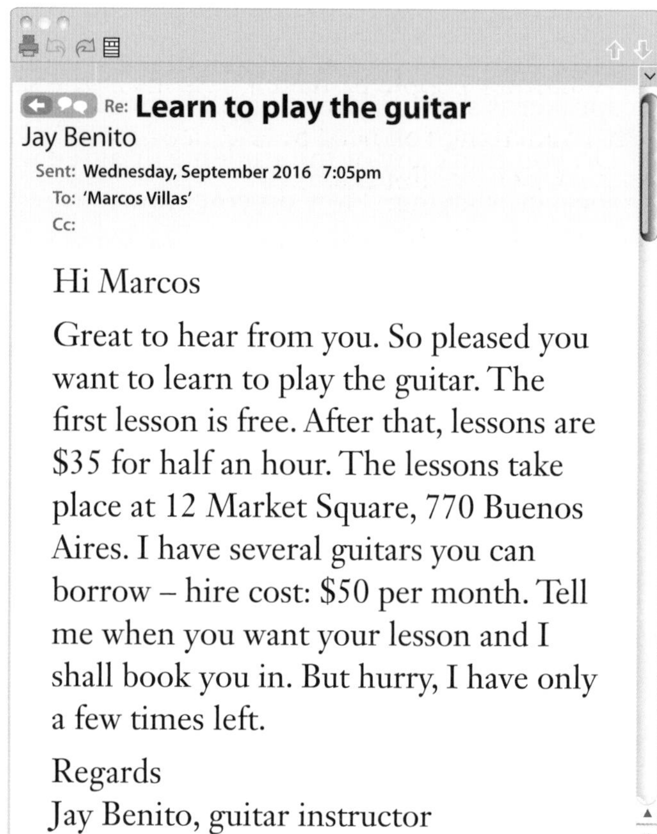

Re: **Learn to play the guitar**
Jay Benito
Sent: Wednesday, September 2016 7:05pm
To: 'Marcos Villas'
Cc:

Hi Marcos

Great to hear from you. So pleased you want to learn to play the guitar. The first lesson is free. After that, lessons are $35 for half an hour. The lessons take place at 12 Market Square, 770 Buenos Aires. I have several guitars you can borrow – hire cost: $50 per month. Tell me when you want your lesson and I shall book you in. But hurry, I have only a few times left.

Regards
Jay Benito, guitar instructor

Understanding

1. What kind of lessons does Jay offer?
2. How much does the first guitar lesson cost?
3. Where does Jay do his teaching?
4. Do you think Marcos is an experienced guitar player? Why/why not?
5. Do you think the information in the advertisement is accurate and clear? In what ways could it have been more accurate and clear?

Writing workshop: Writing an email

You are going to write an email asking for information about the advertisement on the right.

Learn tennis after school!

No experience necessary.

All equipment provided.

Rate: $25 per lesson.

For further information email: Theo Donaldo theodon16@ilios.com

Planning your email

Imagine you want to learn to play tennis and have seen the advertisement above on your school noticeboard. What information do you need to find out? For example:

- Where are the lessons held?
- When are the lessons held – which day and what time?
- How long are the lessons?
- What will you need to wear?
- Will other people be having lessons at the same time?

Is there anything you need to let Theo Donaldo know when you write your email? For example:

- how old you are
- if you have had tennis lessons before
- what time you finish school and which days you are available.

Now think about the kind of language you will use in your email. This is an email to a person who may give you tennis lessons. He is not a friend, so it is best to keep your language quite formal. However, try to use a friendly tone and use words and phrases that will show Theo Donaldo that you are keen to learn tennis.

Writing, editing and proofreading

Now write your email. Remember to ask for all the information you need, explaining clearly what you want to know. Give any information about yourself that you think Theo Donaldo might need to know. Write about 150 words.

When you have finished writing your email, read it through carefully and correct any mistakes in spelling, grammar or punctuation. Now show it to a partner. Can they suggest ways that it can be improved?

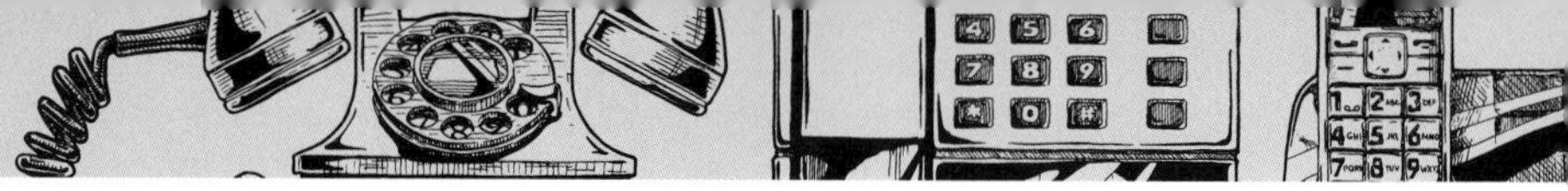

Progress check ✓

1. Who made the first telephone call? (1 mark)

2. A sound that is indistinct is:

   a clear **b** not clear **c** loud (1 mark)

3. Complete the sentences using the correct form of the verbs in brackets.

   a They __________ their friends this weekend. (hope/visit)

   b I shall __________ my book tomorrow. (remember/bring)

   c Please __________ what I am saying. (try/follow) (3 marks)

4. Correct the mistakes in the following sentences.

   a She finished to do her homework.

   b He decided going for a walk. (2 marks)

5. Why might a ship fly the Blue Peter flag? (1 mark)

6. How did the people using semaphore send their messages?

   a by using different coloured flags

   b by holding flags in different positions (1 mark)

7. When were electric traffic lights first used?

   a at the beginning of the nineteenth century

   b at the beginning of the twentieth century (1 mark)

8. Fill in the gaps in the paragraph with words from the box.

off	up	on	out	down

   I got __________ the bus and sat __________ . I looked __________ of the window. When we reached the marketplace I stood __________ and got __________ the bus. (5 marks)

9. Write down four facts about the history of communication that you have learned in this chapter. (4 marks)

10. Write a short email asking for information about an advertisement you have seen for a sports club you are interested in joining. (6 marks)

(Total: 25 marks)

Progress assessment

		🙂	😐	🙁
Reading skills	I can understand the main points in a text.	O	O	O
	I can understand the detail of an argument in a text.	O	O	O
Use of English skills	I can use infinitive forms after verbs and adjectives and -ing forms after verbs and prepositions.	O	O	O
	I can use a range of prepositional verbs and common phrasal verbs.	O	O	O
Listening skills	I can understand most of the detail of an argument when someone is speaking.	O	O	O
	I can recognise typical features of factual information when someone is speaking.	O	O	O
Speaking skills	I can give an opinion on a range of topics.	O	O	O
	I can ask questions to help me understand clearly what someone means.	O	O	O
Writing skills	I can write, edit and proofread written work with some support.	O	O	O
	I can use the appropriate style in my writing.	O	O	O

✓ Action plan

Reading: I need to ____________________

Use of English: I need to ____________________

Listening: I need to ____________________

Speaking: I need to ____________________

Writing: I need to ____________________

I would like to know more about ____________________

Forming comparative adjectives

For information on the use of comparative adjectives, see Unit 1 page 17.

Adjective	Rule	Examples
one syllable (most)	add –er	warmer, taller, quicker
one syllable ending with a silent –e	drop the –e and add –er	larger, nicer, later
one syllable ending with consonant + vowel + consonant	double the final consonant and add –er*	bigger, sadder, wetter
one or two syllables ending with –y	change –y to –i and add –er	drier, luckier, happier
two syllables, not ending with y (many)	'more' + adjective**	more careful, more patient
adjectives with three syllables or more	'more' + adjective	more possible, more expensive, more interesting

* Exception: we don't double the final consonant when an adjective ends in –y or –w; examples: slower, greyer.

** With some two-syllable adjectives, we can use 'more' or add '–er'; examples: cleverer/more clever; simpler/more simple; polite/more polite.

Irregular comparative adjectives

These common adjectives have irregular comparative forms.

Adjective	Comparative
good	better
bad	worse
little (quantity)	less
far	farther/further
well (healthy)	better

Forming adverbs

For information on the use of adverbs, see Unit 4 pages 60–61 and 64–65.

Most adverbs are formed by adding –ly to an adjective.

Adjective	Rule	Examples
most adjectives	add –ly	slowly, carefully, quickly
adjectives ending with –le	remove the –e and add –y	possibly, simply, terribly
adjectives ending with –y	remove –y and add –ily	easily, luckily, happily
adjectives ending with –ic	add –ally*	realistically, enthusiastically, tragically
adjectives ending with –ly	use 'in a … way/manner'	in a silly way, in a friendly manner

* Exception: public → publicly

Irregular adverbs

Some adverbs have the same form as the adjective: hard, fast, straight, late, early, daily, wrong. 'Well' is the adverb that corresponds to the adjective 'good'.

Forming comparative adverbs

For information on the use of comparative adverbs, see Unit 4 page 61.

Adverb	Rule	Examples
adverbs ending with –ly	use 'more' in front of the adverb	more carefully, more patiently
short adverbs that do not end with –ly	add –er if the adverb ends in –e, add –r	faster, harder, later

Irregular comparative adverbs

Adverb	Comparative
well	better
badly	worse
ill	worse
little	less
much	more
far	further/farther

Forming verbs + –ing

Verb	Rule	Examples
most verbs	add –ing	look → looking
verbs ending with consonant + –e	remove the –e and add –ing	move → moving
verbs ending with –ee	add –ing	agree → agreeing
verbs ending with consonant + vowel + consonant	double the final consonant and add –ing*	stop → stopping
verbs ending with –ie	change –ie to –y and add –ing	lie → lying

* Exceptions: We do not double a final –w or –x; examples: flow → flowing, fix → fixing. We do not double the consonant when the last syllable is not stressed; example: order → ordering.

Forming verbs + ed

Verb	Rule	Examples
most verbs	add –ed	look → looked
verbs ending with –e or –ee	add –d	move → moved agree → agreed
verbs ending in consonant + y	change –y to –i and add –ed	study → studied
verbs ending in consonant + vowel + consonant	double the final consonant and add –ed*	stop → stopped prefer → preferred

* Exception: We do not double the consonant when the last syllable is not stressed. Example: order → ordered.

Verb forms

Present simple

See Unit 3 page 44 and Unit 8 page 129.

Positive	I/you/we/they walk	He/she/it walks
Negative	I/you/we/they don't walk	He/she/it doesn't walk
Question	Do I/you/we/they walk?	Does he/she/it walk?

Present continuous

See Unit 3 page 48 and Unit 8 page 129.

Positive	I am walking	He/she/it is walking	You/we/they are walking
Negative	I'm not walking	He/she/it isn't walking	You/we/they aren't walking
Question	Am I walking?	Is he/she/it walking?	Are you/we/they walking?

Past simple

See Unit 3 page 44.

Positive	I/you/he/she/it/we/they walked
Negative	I/you/he/she/it/we/they didn't walk
Question	Did I/you/he/she/it walk?

Past continuous

See Unit 3 page 49.

Positive	I/he/she/it was walking	You/we/they were walking
Negative	I/he/she/it wasn't walking	You/we/they weren't walking
Question	Was I/he/she/it walking?	Were you/we/they walking?

Present perfect simple

See Unit 2 pages 32–33.

Positive	I/you/we/they have walked	He/she/it has walked
Negative	I/you/we/they haven't walked	He/she/it hasn't walked
Question	Have I/you/we/they walked?	Has he/she/it walked?

Past perfect simple

See Unit 8 page 124.

Positive	I/you/he/she/it/we/they had walked
Negative	I/you/he/she/it/we/they hadn't walked
Question	Had I/you/he/she/it/we/they walked?

abstract noun a noun that refers to an idea, quality or concept that cannot be seen, heard, touched, etc. Examples: happiness; truth; beauty. *See also* concrete noun.

active verbs are active when the subject of the sentence (the agent) does the action. Example: He *cleaned* the windows this morning. *See also* passive.

adjective a word that gives more information about a noun or adds to its meaning. Adjectives are often used in front of a noun. Example: They live in a *big* house. Adjectives can also be used after verbs such as 'be', 'feel' and 'look'. Examples: He is *hungry*; She feels *happy*; You look *tired*.

adverb a word that is used to give more information about a verb, adjective or another adverb. Examples: She speaks English *well*; He is *very* tall; He spoke *really* loudly.

auxiliary a verb such as 'be', 'have' or 'do' that is used with a main verb to form tenses, passive forms and questions. Examples: She *is* eating her lunch; She *has* eaten her lunch; Her lunch *was* eaten. *Did* she eat her lunch? *See also* modal verb.

clause a group of words that contains a verb and usually some other words, too. Clauses form part of a sentence or may be complete sentences on their own. Example: I went to school. *See also* conditional clause, relative clause.

command an order to do something. We often use imperative verbs in commands. Example: Stop talking. *See also* imperative.

comparative the form of an adjective or adverb that is used when comparing things. Examples: You are *taller* than me; Mara works *harder* than Jamal.

compound adjective an adjective made up of two or more words. Examples: She is a *prize-winning* writer; He bought a *second-hand* car.

compound noun a noun made up of two or more words. Examples: website, swimming pool.

concrete noun a noun that refers to something that can be seen, heard, touched, etc. Examples: school, house, apple. *See also* abstract noun.

conditional clause a clause that describes something that must happen in order for something else to happen. Conditional clauses usually begin with 'if' or 'unless'. Examples: *If I see her*, I will tell her what you said; *Unless it stops raining*, we will not go for a walk.

conjunction a word that is used to link other words or parts of a sentence, such as 'and', 'but', 'since' and 'as'.

continuous form a verb form used to describe an action that continues over a period of time. We make continuous forms using a form of the verb 'be' with the present participle of the main verb. To change the tense, we change the form of 'be'. Examples: I *am eating* my lunch; He *was reading* his book.

contraction a shortened form of a word or group of words. An apostrophe is used to show where letters have been missed out. Examples: I'm (I am); you're (you are).

countable noun a noun that refers to something that can be counted. Countable nouns have singular and plural forms. Examples: planet/planets; book/books. *See also* uncountable noun.

determiner a word that introduces a noun and forms part of a noun phrase. Examples: a/an, the, this, some, many, this, that, these, much, your.

direct speech the words spoken by someone and quoted in writing. To indicate direct speech, we use inverted commas, or speech marks. Example: She said, *"I will see you tomorrow." See also* reported speech.

future a verb form used to refer to something that has not yet happened. To talk about something that has been arranged in the future, we often use the present simple or present continuous. Examples: My piano lesson is at 4 o'clock. I am having a piano lesson tomorrow.

gerund a present participle of a verb when it is used as a noun. Example: I like *reading*.

imperative a verb form that expresses a command or instruction. Examples: *Be* quiet; *Close* the door; *Stir* the mixture carefully.

infinitive the basic form of a verb. Examples: read, be. The infinitive with 'to' is 'to' + base form: 'to read', 'to be'.

–ing form the present participle form of a verb ending in –ing. We use the –ing form in continuous forms. Example: I *am reading* a book. We also use –ing forms as nouns (gerunds). Examples: I like *reading*; *Reading* is relaxing. We also some use –ing forms as adjectives. Example: This is an *exciting* book.

irregular an irregular word does not follow the normal rules. Irregular nouns do not have plurals that end in –s. Examples: man → men; child → children. An irregular verb does not have a past tense and past participle that end in –ed. Examples: go → went/gone; be → was/were/been. *See also* regular.

main verb the verb that expresses the main meaning in a clause (unlike an auxiliary verb). Main verbs can be used with or without an auxiliary verb. Examples: I *read* a good book last week. I am *reading* a good book.

modal verb an auxiliary verb that we can use with another verb to express ideas such as ability, advice, possibility, permission, etc. The main modal verbs are: can, could, may might, must, ought (to), shall, should, will and would. Examples: He *can* play the piano very well; You *should* wear a coat; He *might* visit you next week. You *can* borrow my phone.

noun a word that refers to a person, animal, thing or idea. *See also* abstract noun, compound noun, concrete noun, countable noun, noun phrase, uncountable noun.

noun phrase a phrase that contains a noun. Noun phrases can contain determiners such as 'a/an' or 'the' and other words that give more information about the noun. Example: Have you seen *the blue shirt that I was wearing yesterday?*

object a noun or pronoun that is the person or thing that is affected by a verb. Example: He kicked *the ball* into the goal. *See also* subject.

participle *See* –ing form, past participle.

passive verbs are passive when the subject of the verb has the action done to it. Example: The windows *were cleaned* last week. *See also* active.

past continuous *See* continuous form.

past participle a form of a verb that we use to make some past forms and passives. Regular verbs have past participles that end in –ed. Examples: He has *delivered* all the leaflets; The windows were *cleaned* yesterday. Irregular verbs have different forms. Example: I have *sent* my friend a postcard. Past participles are also used to form adjectives. Example: They have mended the *broken* window.

past perfect (simple) a verb form that we make with 'had' and the past participle. We use the past perfect to talk about an event that happened before another event in the past. Example: The film *had* already *started* when we got to the cinema. We also use the past perfect in reported statements. Example: She said she *had* just *arrived*.

past simple a verb form that we make by adding –ed to regular verbs. Irregular verbs have different forms. We use the past simple to talk about actions or events that happened in the past. Example: I *called* him yesterday.

past tense *See* continuous form, past perfect, past simple, tense.

phrasal verb a verb made up of a verb and a particle such as 'to', 'in' 'up', 'off', 'down', etc. A phrasal verb often has a different meaning from the verb alone. When a phrasal verb has an object, it can usually come before or after the particle. Examples: My car *broke down;* He *put on* his coat.

phrase a group of words that forms a unit within a clause. Examples: Have you seen *my blue coat;* I put the book *on the table*.

plural the form of a word that we use to refer to more than one person or thing. Examples: books; they.

preposition a word such as 'at', 'into', 'on' or 'for' that we use before a noun or pronoun to show place, direction, time, method, etc. Examples: The book is *on* the desk; He walked *across* the street; I will see you *at* 6 o'clock; I went to Japan *by* plane.

prepositional verb a verb that is made up of a verb and a preposition. Prepositional verbs always have objects and we cannot separate the verb and the preposition. Examples: She *listened to* what her friend was saying. He cannot *do without* your help.

present continuous *See* continuous form.

present participle *See* –ing form.

present perfect (simple) the verb form that we make with a form of 'have' and the past participle of the main verb. The present perfect has many uses. For example, it is used to talk about something that started in the past and continues in the present. Example: She *has lived* in Paris for over ten years.

present simple the form of a verb that we use to talk about things that are true in the present and actions that happen regularly in the present. We make the present simple with the base form of the verb. With 'he', 'she' and 'it' we add –s to the base form of regular verbs and many irregular verbs. Examples: He *lives* in Hong Kong; I often *walk* to school. We also use the present simple to talk about something that is fixed in the future. Example: My lesson *starts* at 6 o'clock.

present tense *See* present simple, present perfect, continuous form, tense.

pronoun a word that is used in place of a noun. Subject pronouns usually come before a verb. Examples: I, you, he, she, it, we, they. Object pronouns come after the verb. Examples: me, you, him, her, it, us, them. Relative pronouns connect relative clauses to main clauses in a sentence. Examples: who, which, that. Possessive pronouns show who something belongs to. Examples: mine, yours, his, hers, ours, theirs.

quantifier a word that expresses the quantity, number or amount of something. Examples: all, both, many, several, lots of, little.

regular a word such as a noun or verb that follows normal rules. For example, regular nouns have plurals with –s, and regular verbs have past participles ending in –ed.

relative clause a clause that gives information about someone or something in the main clause. A relative clause is connected to a main clause by a relative pronoun such as 'that', 'which', 'who' or 'where'. Example: I read the book *that my friend lent me*.

reported speech the words someone uses to report what someone has said. Example: She said that she enjoyed the match. *See also* direct speech.

sentence a group of words that expresses a complete thought and makes complete sense. Sentences contain a main verb, begin with a capital letter and end with a full stop, exclamation mark or question mark. Examples: Paulo is playing football; That is great! Why did you do that?

perfect *See* present perfect and past perfect.

singular the form of a word that we use to refer to one person or thing. Examples: book; she.

statement a sentence that is not a question or a command. Example: The match has just started.

subject the person or thing that performs the action of a verb in a sentence. Example: *He* kicked the ball into the goal. *See also* object.

syllable a word or part of a word that contains one vowel sound and usually one or more consonants before or after the vowel sound. Example: meet (one syllable); meeting (two syllables 'meet' and 'ing').

tense the form that a verb takes to show when something happened or when someone did something. In English, there are two main tenses: present and past. There are four forms of the present tense: the present simple, present continuous, present perfect and present perfect continuous. There are four forms of the past tense: past simple, past continuous, past perfect and past perfect continuous.

uncountable noun a noun that refers to something that we cannot count. Uncountable nouns do not have a plural form. Examples: water, information. *See also* countable noun.

verb a word that describes what someone or something does, or what happens. Examples: look, read, seem, understand.